Praise for
The Best Boy in the United States of America: A Memoir of Blessings and Kisses

"With humor and honesty, Wolfson reminds us that mensches are not born—they are made by an incredible village of loving people. A must-read for everyone trying to raise a mensch!"

—**Rabbi Sherre Hirsch**, spiritual life consultant at Canyon Ranch; spiritual commentator, *The Today Show*

"Funny in tone, snappy in style—a leisurely read that makes important points about growing up Jewish and the task of preserving Jewish identity."

—**Rabbi Lawrence A. Hoffman**, editor, *My People's Prayer Book: Traditional Prayers, Modern Commentaries* series

"This warm, hilarious and deeply moving story of relationships will resonate powerfully with all those 'best boys' (and best girls) who grew up in post-war America ... and leave the rest of us wishing we had grown up alongside the author in the American heartland."

—**Rabbi Julie Schonfeld**, executive vice president, the Rabbinical Assembly

"An engaging and heartfelt love story—love of home, love of family, love of community and love of the Jewish people."

—**Abraham H. Foxman**, national director, Anti-Defamation League

"A charming reminder from a master storyteller of the power of our family stories to teach, inspire and remind us of what really matters in life."

—**Lee M. Hendler**, author, *The Year Mom Got Religion: One Woman's Midlife Journey into Judaism*

"An homage to fabulous storytelling, a homespun combination of family, love, hilarity and poignancy only a Jew from Omaha could summon up."

—**Robin Kramer**, executive director, Reboot, an incubator of Jewish arts and culture

"A touching celebration of the power of family to raise up souls and heal the world. With wisdom and heart, Ron Wolfson offers the perfect antidote to the sour pessimism that afflicts contemporary Jewish life."
—**Rabbi Edward Feinstein**, Valley Beth Shalom, Encino, California; author, *The Chutzpah Imperative* and *Tough Questions Jews Ask*

"A magic story, one filled with values and love.... Charmingly captures the story of [Ron Wolfson's] life from his childhood in Omaha to his current roles of educator, husband, parent and grandparent.... This book is a delight!"
—**Rabbi David Ellenson**, chancellor emeritus, Hebrew Union College–Jewish Institute of Religion; acting director, Schusterman Center for Israel Studies; visiting professor, Brandeis University

"Want to know the secret of becoming a legendary teacher, sought-after public speaker and Jewish educator extraordinaire? You can find the answer between the covers of this book!"
—**Harlene Appelman**, executive director, the Covenant Foundation

"A great reminder of why families are so important, and it's a fun book to read!"
—**Rick Warren**, pastor, Saddleback Church; author, *The Purpose-Driven Life*

"A vivid and heartwarming memoir ... filled with the love and warmth of an incredible family for whom Judaism is an essential part of who they are."
—**Rabbi Mike Uram**, executive director and campus rabbi, Penn Hillel, University of Pennsylvania

"Ron Wolfson is the Mark Twain of the Jewish community."
—**Scott Seigel**, president, Temple Bat Yahm, Newport Beach

"Ever the storyteller, Ron invites us into his Jewish journey, a journey filled with laughter, tears and insights."
—**Allan Finkelstein**, president emeritus, JCC Association of North America

The Best Boy
in
the United States
of America

Other Books by Dr. Ron Wolfson

Relational Judaism
Using the Power of Relationships to Transform the Jewish Community

God's To-Do List
103 Ways to Be an Angel and Do God's Work on Earth

Be Like God
God's To-Do List for Kids

The Seven Questions You're Asked in Heaven
Reviewing and Renewing Your Life on Earth

The Spirituality of Welcoming
How to Transform Your Congregation into a Sacred Community

What You Will See Inside a Synagogue
(co-authored with Rabbi Lawrence A. Hoffman, PhD)

The Art of Jewish Living Series

Hanukkah, 2nd Ed.
The Family Guide to Spiritual Celebration

Passover, 2nd Ed.
The Family Guide to Spiritual Celebration
(with Joel Lurie Grishaver)

Shabbat, 2nd Ed.
The Family Guide to Preparing for and Celebrating the Sabbath

A Time to Mourn, a Time to Comfort, 2nd Ed.
A Guide to Jewish Bereavement

The Best Boy
in *the* United States
of America

A MEMOIR

OF BLESSINGS AND KISSES

Dr. Ron Wolfson

For People of All Faiths, All Backgrounds

JEWISH LIGHTS Publishing

Woodstock, Vermont

The Best Boy in the United States of America:
A Memoir of Blessings and Kisses

2015 Hardcover Edition, First Printing
© 2015 by Ron Wolfson

Gribenes photo courtesy of Tori Avey, food writer and recipe developer at ToriAvey.com. Excerpts from *Let's Talk About God* by Dorothy K. Kripke, *z"l*, reprinted courtesy of Torah Aura Productions. "Dear Old Nebraska U. (There Is No Place Like Nebraska)," words and music by Harry Pecha, © 1931 (renewed) Edwin H. Morris & Company, a division of MPL Music Publishing, Inc., all rights reserved. Reprinted by permission of Hal Leonard Corporation.

For information regarding permission to reprint material from this book, please mail or fax your request in writing to Jewish Lights Publishing, Permissions Department, at the address / fax number listed below, or email your request to permissions@jewishlights.com.

Library of Congress Cataloging-in-Publication Data
Wolfson, Ron, author.
  The best boy in the United States of America : a memoir of blessings and kisses / Dr. Ron Wolfson.
      pages cm
  ISBN 978-1-58023-838-0 (hardcover)—ISBN 978-1-58023-844-1 (ebook)
1. Wolfson, Ron. 2. Jews—United States—Biography. I. Title.
  E184.37.W66A3 2015
  973'.04924—dc23
                                        2015012045
  10 9 8 7 6 5 4 3 2 1

Manufactured in the United States of America
Cover and interior design: Tim Holtz
Cover art: flag image © Sergey Kamshylin/Shutterstock

For People of All Faiths, All Backgrounds
Jewish Lights Publishing
A Division of LongHill Partners, Inc.
Sunset Farm Offices, Route 4, P.O. Box 237
Woodstock, VT 05091
Tel: (802) 457-4000 Fax: (802) 457-4004
www.jewishlights.com

For S. K.

Contents

The Best Boy in the United States of America

I am the best boy in the United States of America.

That's what my grandfather—my "Zaydie"—called me from the time I was a little child in Omaha, Nebraska. I know it's true because this is a true story. All my stories are true.

Zaydie is Yiddish for "grandfather," but it means much more than that. It is a term of endearment that is wrapped in love like a warm fuzzy blanket on a cold winter's night. Zaydie's name was Louis Paperny, but everyone (besides his grandchildren) called him "Louie."

Zaydie was short of stature, maybe five feet tall—but stocky of build, with an expressive face featuring sparkling blue bug-eyes and an always ruddy complexion. He was stronger than an ox. His early years as a fruit and vegetable peddler lugging heavy sacks of potatoes endowed him with huge arms and legs. And yet he was one of the most gentle of human beings. He wore his emotions on his sleeve—a man who easily cried at the drop of a hat and certainly at the sight of a grandchild.

Zaydie loved three things: his family, his business, and his adopted country—the United States of America. I never, ever heard Zaydie say "the United States." It was always "da United States of America," in his thick Russian accent. He embraced the freedom and the opportunity that America afforded him; and woe to anyone who criticized anything about "mine United States of America."

Family lore has it that he left Russia for a girl he had fallen in love with in Minsk, his *basherte* (intended one), a young woman named Ida Wolfson. Ida had immigrated to the United States of America a few years earlier, and once Louis Paperny saved enough kopeks, he booked passage to the New World. He found Ida in Omaha and married her, and they began to build their family.

Zaydie's peddler wagon became a roadside stand that eventually gave way to a modern supermarket and liquor store—Louis Market (but everyone called it "Louie's" Market)—in a neighborhood called Benson. The fact that he was able to raise a family (four girls, the baby was my mother), build a successful business, and enjoy a level of affluence he never believed possible—all this he credited to the United States of America, "da greatest country in the void."

As a little boy, I loved going over to Bubbie (grandmother) and Zaydie's. We would pull into the driveway of 2619 North 56th Street, right next to a huge evergreen tree that dominated the backyard, and my brothers, Bobby and Dougie, and I would spill out, anxious to see if Zaydie was back from the store. I knew he was home if his enormous, shiny Packard was in the one-car garage.

Bubbie was always home—it was her domain. Sometimes she would be out in the yard, pulling freshly dried *gotkes* (underwear) from the clothesline, placing them carefully into her basket. Sometimes she would be in her tiny kitchen, the entrance to which was just inside the back door to Bubbie and Zaydie's home, opening directly into Bubbie's realm.

After a kiss from my grandmother, I'd grab a handful of "Bubbie's cookies"—mandel bread studded with walnuts and sparkling with cinnamon sugar—and run through the dining room and into the living room, where Zaydie awaited.

Zaydie ruled from a big overstuffed red velvet chair in his living room, where he sat like a king, watching his big-screen TV. Once Zaydie made some money, he always bought the biggest, newest television set, including the first color TV in Omaha. Right next to the chair was a side table where he kept three things: a pack of cigarettes (unfiltered Camels—he smoked four packs a day), his sterling silver Ronson lighter, and a glass of water for his teeth. There was no ashtray; Zaydie put the butts out in the arms of his big red chair, the upholstery pockmarked with dozens of burn holes. You should have seen the dashboard of his Packard; how he didn't burn down the house or blow up the car is a small miracle!

Rounding the corner into the living room, I would run toward Zaydie sitting on his throne. His ruddy face would brighten like a red stoplight, but his open arms signaled go, go, go. Rushing into his arms, turning my face toward his barrel chest, I submitted to his hug, smelling the smoke on his breath, looking up at his bug-eyed blue peepers that seemed always on the verge of spilling tears of joy.

Just then, he did it: Zaydie would cross his powerful legs behind me like a World Wrestling Federation brawler, locking me in a tight embrace. He planted a huge, scratchy, sloppy wet kiss on my lips and wrapped his enormous arms around my back. I wriggled to try to escape his grasp, screaming, "Zaydie, Zaydie, let me go, let me go!" But it was no use. I was a prisoner of his love. When I finally settled down into his loving hug, he looked me straight in the eye and said, "Ronnie, you're da best boy in da United States of America! *Da best boy in da United States of A-mer-ee-ca!*" I struggled some more, wanting and never wanting him to let me out. "Ronnie, you're da *best boy in da United States of A-mer-ee-ca!*" "I know, Zaydie, I know, let me go!" Zaydie wasn't satisfied until he said it a third time: "Ronnie, you're da *best boy in da United States of A-mer-ee-ca!*" and then, finally, he loosened his legs and I escaped.

And when my younger brother Bobby rounded the corner, running into Zaydie's arms, and Zaydie put him in the dreaded/beloved leg lock, and Zaydie would give him a huge, scratchy, sloppy wet kiss right on his lips, and wrap Bobby in his enormous arms, look him straight in the eye, and say, "Bobby, you're da best boy in da United States of America! *Da United States of A-mer-ee-ca!*"—it mattered not which of us he held. And when my brother Dougie jumped into Zaydie's lap, Zaydie would put *him* in the leg lock, and give him a huge, scratchy, sloppy wet kiss right on his lips, and wrap Dougie in his enormous arms, look him straight in the eye, and say, "Dougie, you're da best boy in da United States of America! *Da United States of A-mer-ee-ca!*"—it mattered not. And when cousin Laurie Luttbeg jumped into Zaydie's lap, and Zaydie put her in a leg lock, and gave her a huge, scratchy, sloppy wet kiss right on her lips, and wrapped Laurie in his enormous arms, and looked her straight in the eye and said, "Laurie, you're da best girl in da United States of America! *Da United States of A-mer-ee-ca!*"—it mattered not.

Because for Louie Paperny, each one of his nine *aineklach,* his grandchildren, was the best boy or the best girl in the United States of America. We believed him. I believed him. And in a certain way, I've lived the rest of my life trying to be that best boy.

The big evergreen tree and the back door to the kitchen

The Best Boy in the United States of America ... Except in Religious School

Did you go to religious school as a kid? My Christian friends went to Sunday school; my Mormon friends went to religious instruction at 6:30 a.m. weekday mornings before public school. I went to Hebrew school, Monday and Wednesday, 4:00 to 6:00 p.m.

Did you have Mr. Friedman? I had the same teacher in Hebrew school for three years in a row—*bet, gimel,* and *dalet* class—second, third, and fourth grade. Let's call him "Mr. Friedman."

He wasn't really a Hebrew school teacher. He really sold appliances at Sears. But, he had a good *neshoma,* a good soul, and he knew some Hebrew, and he was willing to come to Beth El Synagogue in Omaha, Nebraska, every afternoon to try to teach me and my friends a few Hebrew words. He knew nothing about teaching, and he had no classroom management skills. He spoke in a high-pitched voice, with a thick Old-Country accent that we kids determined was most definitely Lithuanian.

Hebrew school was boring. I was a good student at Dundee School. But the last place I wanted to be at four in the afternoon after a full day in public school was another classroom. I wanted to be home watching cartoons, or playing ball, or ogling Annette Funicello on *The Mickey Mouse Club.* But Mondays and Wednesdays, my friends and I would walk from Dundee School, past Cris Rexall

Drug, up Dodge Street, past the candy shop that sold my favorite sugar dots on long, narrow strips of paper, and enter Beth El from Forty-Eighth Street into the social hall, where there was a makeshift gym for us kids to blow off some steam. Some gym. The big piece of equipment was a long ladder-like set of parallel bars that served as a basketball hoop. We played for fifteen, twenty minutes until the bell rang, and we raced upstairs to room two, where Friedman awaited in his short-sleeved white shirt and paisley tie.

Friedman began each lesson the same way: "Velcome to room t-ewe!" emphasizing the word "two" as if he were spitting on the floor. Truth be told, I was happy to be sitting according to the alphabetical seating chart, in the back of the room, next to Mark (Moshe) Zalkin—less likely to be showered with Friedman's expectorant.

What a room! At Dundee School, the classrooms were lined with colorful bulletin boards and posters. At Beth El Hebrew School, room t-ewe had one tan cork bulletin board with exactly one thing tacked on it: a Jewish calendar from the *chevrah kadisha* (mortuary). With its four rows of classroom desks with names and doodles carved in the top by bored kids and a hissing radiator huffing and puffing to keep the place warm in the cold Nebraska winter, room two was a dreadful place to spend a long afternoon learning a foreign language.

Friedman didn't help matters with his teaching techniques. His idea of an exciting lesson: Hebrew speed-reading drills. "You, Volfson, you sit here in da front of da room. You vill try to read faster than Moshe. Moshe, you sit next to Volfson." Then Friedman would pull out a stopwatch. "Okay, boy-es [it didn't matter that half the class was girls], ven I say 'Go!' I vant you should read as fast as you can! *Echad, shtayim, shalosh* [1, 2, 3] ... go!" I read as fast as I could and so did Moshe. Whoever got to the end of the paragraph first was the winner. This was exciting at 5:30 in the afternoon?

So in Hebrew school I became a class clown. I'd do anything to get Friedman off topic and furious: spitballs, notes to friends, sneaking a peek at comic books underneath the desktop, throwing pencils into the acoustical tile ceiling, talking—always talking. Friedman would try to control the classroom by yelling and threatening. "Volfson, you, geet out!"—the harbinger of a wonderful respite at the principal's office or sometimes Rabbi Kripke's study. "Volfson, I call your parents!"—a threat that he actually followed through with only once. Most of the time he would begrudgingly put up with my antics. Friedman had a name for me; he called me *vildeh chayeh*—that's Yiddish for "wild animal." So most afternoons at Hebrew school, under his breath, Friedman would mumble, "Volfson, you *vildeh chayeh* you."

When he got really upset, Friedman would yell at me—loudly—a single Hebrew word: "*Sheket! Sheket! SHEKET SHEKET SHEKET!*"

Do you know what it means? I had no idea. The literal translation is "quiet," but the way Friedman shouted the word, it means "Shut up!" "Shut up, you ungrateful *vildeh chayeh*, you!"

"*Sheket! Sheket! Sheket!*" That's all I heard all afternoon. "*SHEKET!*" Not once did I get a "*Sheket b'vakashah!*"—"Shut up *please!*" It was the only Hebrew word I learned in those three years.

Well, I thought I learned it. When I went for my first Bar Mitzvah lesson, the tutor—Mr. Katz, another sweet man from Europe—pinched my cheek as the old-timers did and asked, "Sonny, vat's your name in Hebrew?"

I said, "*Sheket!*" (For the longest time I thought my Hebrew name was "Sheket ben Avraham.")

If Freidman got really upset, he would curse me out in Yiddish, which of course he mangled into English so I would understand it. He got beet red in the face and yelled at the top of his lungs, "You, Volfson! Go to da back of da room and spit in your own face!"

I had no idea what he was talking about.[*] I was nine years old, so I'd stand up, defiant, throw my head back, and try it. Pooey! Pooey!

---

[*] The Yiddish curse is "*Shpie in punim.*" You may have heard the expression *shayna punim*, "a sweet face." This is the opposite.

I suppose now is the time to reveal that as I write this, I am completing forty years as a professor of Jewish education. I travel the world teaching Jewish educators, rabbis, lay leaders, and communal professionals how to improve their classrooms, schools, synagogues, community centers, Hillels, summer camps, and Federations. I have written thirteen books, many of them guides to bringing Judaism alive in a joyous and meaningful way in the home. I give at least a hundred talks a year about Jewish life, making my points by telling these stories—did I mention that all of them are true?

Anyway, my reputation as a *vildeh chayeh* at Beth El might have been the reason it took my synagogue twenty years to invite me back to Omaha to give a lecture on Jewish education. I had already published four best-selling books about Jewish life, and my mother, Bernice, ensured that a big crowd showed up. The talk was a blast to give, and of course it was very well received by my hometown friends and family. Guess who was sitting in the front row? Yep. At the end of the evening, Mr. Friedman stood up with a huge smile on his face, turned to the assembled group, and in that unforgettable, high-pitched Lithuanian-accented voice proclaimed, "Ronnie Volfson vas the best student I ever had in Hebrew school!"

Bubbie's Candles

The best time at Bubbie's and Zaydie's was celebrating Shabbat. Bubbie would rise at five in the morning on Fridays to begin preparing for her huge weekly Shabbat dinner.

My first memory of those days is newspapers on the floor. The first thing Bubbie did was wash her kitchen floor. Now this made no sense whatsoever. She'd be cooking all day long, and the floor would get dirty. After she washed the floor, she did something even more curious—she lined it with newspapers ... newspapers covering the entire floor of her kitchen. (She always used the *Omaha World Herald* for this purpose—never the *Forverts*, her beloved Yiddish newspaper.)

I never understood why Bubbie and the women of that era began their Shabbat preparations by washing the floor. I thought it was part of the Jewish ritual. Only as a college student did I finally figure it out. Bubbie knew that the time to begin Shabbat would likely come upon her quickly; by traditional Jewish law, the candles are lit eighteen minutes before sundown. In her rush to finish preparing the meal, she wouldn't have time to wash the floor before *bensching licht* (candle lighting). The only solution: wash the floor *first* thing in the morning, and cover it with newspapers to catch the inevitable drippings. Then, just before lighting her candles, she could simply gather up the newspapers, throw them away, and her nice clean floor would be ready for Shabbes (Yiddish for Shabbat, day of rest). Brilliant!

Bubbie was a tiny little woman, maybe four foot nine, but she was a powerhouse who ruled the roost. She loved having the entire *mishpoche* (family) over for Friday night dinner. When it came time to welcome in Shabbat, Bubbie walked all by herself from the kitchen into the dining room to her breakfront, a huge piece of furniture with cabinets holding all of her precious crystal and china. On the front shelf of the breakfront was a large silver candelabrum with branches for six candles. Why six? Two for the minimum for Shabbat and one for each of her four children: Sylvia, Rose, Ruth, and my mother, Bernice. Bubbie would open a top drawer and pull out six candles and a small black lace scarf, called in Yiddish a *tichel.* She gently placed the *tichel* on top of her head and arranged the candles in the candelabrum. She struck a match, lit the candles, and then did what to me as a young child always seemed very mysterious: Bubbie circled the flames with her hands three times. At the end of the third wave, she covered her eyes, blocking the candles from her sight. She then went into a kind of trance, mumbling a few Hebrew words, all the while slightly moving her tiny body in place, a kind of spiritual aerobics. She held her hands in front of her eyes for what seemed like hours but was in reality only a few moments. She said nothing out loud, but it appeared she was deep in prayer. When she was ready, she lowered her hands from in front of her eyes, and what I would see next has stayed with me ever since. There were always, always, always, every single Shabbat eve, tears streaming down her cheeks. Why was she crying? Much later I understood: Bubbie was talking to God, praying for blessings of good health and success for her family and friends; this was her private spiritual moment of the week.

And then, Bubbie rushed into the adjacent living room, looking for the first grandchild she could get her hands on. Often it was me. I knew what was coming. She would grab me in a warm embrace and plant a big, wet, slobbery, scratchy kiss on my *punim—* it was scratchy because Bubbie had a mole with a little hair sticking out just above her lip—and she would say, "*Guht Shabbes, tateleh* (sweetie), *guht Shabbes!*"

At that moment, I learned the most important lesson I ever learned—or taught—concerning Jewish family life: it's about the blessings *and* the kisses. The rituals without the kisses are empty.

Bubbie lighting candles at Passover

Why Do I Do
What I Do?

The challenge, of course, is maintaining traditions like this from generation to generation. Did Bubbie have any idea why she was doing the ritual in this way, waving her hands over the flames, blocking her sight of the candles? I doubt it. She did it that way because *her* mother lit candles that way. Her *grandmother* most likely lit her candles that way. This was how she had always seen it done, and so this was how she did it.

Once I was invited for Shabbat dinner at the home of my friends Diane and Lenny. Diane, a thirtysomething, very smart trial attorney, was raised in a Jewish home filled with tradition. When it came time to light the Shabbat candles, she began the ritual much as my Bubbie did: set up two four-inch-tall white "utility" tapers on her brass candlesticks, covered her head with a small scarf, and struck a match to light the wicks. When she blew out the match, she looked at the flames and began to circle them with her hands, but as she did, she said something I had never heard before. She began to mumble three words that were barely distinguishable, but they sounded like this: "*Breekh breekh shmay!*" "*Breekh breekh shmay!*" she said again. And again. Three times, each time louder: "*Breekh breekh shmay!*" The first book I wrote was a 280-page guide about the Shabbat dinner ritual, but never, never had I ever heard anyone light candles and scream, "*Breekh breekh shmay!*"

Now, when I am invited to someone's home, I try to be a gracious guest. So I said nothing to Diane about her strange ritual. But as we were saying our good-byes at the end of the evening, I could not help myself.

"Diane," I began, "what a lovely evening! Thanks so much for inviting us." And then I added, in a slightly higher pitched voice, "I just have *one little question.* When you circled the Shabbat candles, you said something like *'Breekh breekh shmay.'* What was that?"

Diane looked me straight in the eye and said, "I don't know."

"Then, why did you say it?"

Diane immediately answered, "My mother lights candles that way, my *grandmother* lit candles that way."

Hearing her response, I was reminded of the well-worn story of the newlywed preparing her first roast for dinner. She puts the ninety-eight-dollar kosher piece of meat on a cutting board, takes a cleaver in hand, and lops off one end of the roast and throws it away, then the other end ... and throws it away. Her new husband is watching this unfold and can't believe his eyes. "Excuse me, what are you doing?"

His wife replies, "I'm preparing the roast."

"But you're throwing half of it away! Why are you doing this?"

Now defensive, the wife replies, "My mother does it this way."

The husband is nonplussed. "Call your mother and ask her what's going on!"

The wife calls. "Mom, I'm making my first roast, and I'm doing it just like you. I cut off one end and threw it away, then the other end and threw it away. Why am I doing it that way?"

The mother laughs, "Oh, honey. When you were a little girl, we had a tiny oven with a roasting pan so small I couldn't get the whole roast in. So I cut off the two ends and put them in *another* pan."

So now I ask Diane, "Do you have any idea what *breekh breekh shmay* means?"

"Not a clue."

"Okay. Slow it down. Maybe I can figure it out."

She says, *"Bareekh shemay."*

"Ah," I say. "It's Aramaic. You're saying the Hebrew equivalent *Barukh sh'mo*!"

A brief explanation: In Jewish public prayer, when the cantor sings the opening formula of a blessing, *Barukh atah Adonai* (Blessed are You, God), the congregation is supposed to respond, *Barukh hu u'varukh sh'mo* (literally, "Blessed is He and blessed is His name"). But in all my travels, I've never actually heard any congregation sing that. Everyone is in such a hurry. I've been in synagogues where the people sing, *Barukh-hu-v'rukh-sh'mo*. Or some contract it to *Barukh-hu-sh'mo*. Or even, *Barukh-sh'mo*. I was in one shul (synagogue) where the cantor in a mellifluous voice sang, *Barukh atah Adonai*, and everyone yelled "*Shmo!*" I don't know who they were talking about—the cantor, the rabbi ... the president, maybe?

So somewhere in the long lineage of Diane's family, someone had the really lovely idea to embellish the ritual of lighting Shabbat candles by whispering this well-known phrase from Jewish tradition while circling the flames three times: *Barukh hu u'varukh sh'mo. Barukh hu u'varukh sh'mo. Barukh hu u'varukh sh'mo.* But over the generations, it turned into *Breekh breekh shmay! Breekh breekh shmay! Breekh breekh shmay!*

Just like Diane, I am sure Bubbie did not know why she danced this beautiful choreography of ritual as she lit her candles. Does it matter, I wonder? Does it matter that she didn't know that the circling of the lights probably comes from the mystics of Tzfat in northern Israel who developed the *Kabbalat Shabbat* prayers? Was it important that she know that she waved her hands over the candles three times because the number three is important in the mystical tradition? Did she know that the motion is supposed to bring the aura of the Shabbat lights into your spiritual consciousness?

No and yes. No, it didn't matter that Bubbie did not know the *reasons* for her ritual; she had found the *meaning* in it. She understood its purpose: to mark the beginning of the Sabbath day, to continue a tradition handed down from generation to generation (*l'dor va-dor*), and perhaps most importantly, to give herself a few minutes of meditation and prayer, her weekly moment of spirituality. Bubbie rarely went to the synagogue to pray to God, but she would never miss her weekly appointment to *talk* with God. I realized all that by watching Bubbie do her ritual.

But yes, it did matter to me that I understood why I was doing what I was doing as I began to embrace Jewish ritual practice. I found myself wanting to do the ritual correctly. Which candle do you light first? Unlike Hanukkah candles (which, as you face the menorah, you set from right to left but light from left to right, honoring that night's candle by lighting it first with the *shammash*, the servant candle), with Shabbat candles it doesn't matter. Why are they white? Symbolic of the joy of Shabbat. I wanted to know these answers for myself, to figure out the relationship between the form of the ritual and the content, to deepen my understanding and commitment to continuing the traditions, and eventually to share this knowledge with the Dianes I would meet as I set off down the road to becoming a Jewish educator.

I met plenty of Dianes. One was the mother of a Bat Mitzvah I met when I served as scholar-in-residence in a large Reform congregation. Just before the Friday night service was to begin, the rabbi invited the family members having honors during the ceremony the next morning into his study so he could write down their Hebrew names. A few of the old-timers knew their Hebrew names, but more than one had forgotten. The rabbi, eager not to embarrass anyone, gave these forgetful folks a Hebrew name on the spot: a middle-aged Bruce became Barukh, a teenage Tiffany became Tirtzah. Finally, the rabbi asked the mother of the Bat Mitzvah girl, "What's your Hebrew name?"

The mother replied, "I don't know my name in Hebrew, but I know it in Yiddish."

The rabbi smiled. "Great, we can use that. What's your Yiddish name?"

In all seriousness, she said, "Brontosaurus."

I thought the rabbi would completely lose it.

But he kept his composure, and upon further inquiry it was determined that the mother's Yiddish name was Branka Sureh, which, for obvious lack of use, had turned into "Brontosaurus."*

It will be difficult to continue Jewish traditions if we think we've been named after dinosaurs and make blessings like a chicken. My job has been to lovingly—and with good-natured humor—explain these practices to those I meet along the way.

---

* Reminds me of the rumor that Steven Spielberg was going to make a Jewish version of *Jurassic Park* called *Dine a Tzouris and Mine a Tzouris* (Your Trouble and My Trouble).

Eat! Eat!

It turns out that food was a way into Judaism for me, beginning with Bubbie's Shabbat dinner. Bubbie Ida was not a good cook—she was a great cook. What came out of her tiny oven was an amazing array of dishes, many of them tailor-made for each member of the family and crafted without the benefit of recipes or cookbooks. No, her major culinary skill can be described with the great Yiddish expression *shitarayn* (pour it in)—"I put a little salt, a little pepper, until it tastes *guht*," Bubbie would say.

Zaydie loved Bubbie's *lukhshen* kugel—noodles, eggs, oil ... period. No sugar. No cinnamon. No cottage cheese. No raisins. Just straight noodles, oven baked until the oil sizzled the top and bottom layers reached a golden brown crispiness, like *tadik* in the Persian tradition. A hunk of kugel sprinkled with salt—heaven! Uncle Mort, Aunt Sylvia's husband, loved Bubbie's Jewish take on osso bucco—oxtails, drowning in thick gravy. Uncle Ben, Aunt Rose's husband, favored the homemade beet borscht, served with a boiled potato and a dab of sour cream. Don Greenberg, Cousin Nancy's husband, was a soup guy—chicken soup with matzah balls served in a huge soup tureen was his favorite. My dad, Alan, ate all of Bubbie's cooking but especially liked the *airlach*, unfertilized eggs hard-boiled in the soup, and *pipiks*, chicken gizzards, little bow ties of hard, grizzled innards that softened in the boiling water.

And me? I loved it all.

I was a fat little boy. There is no other way to describe me. My clothes were purchased in the "husky" section of the department store. For my Bar Mitzvah reception, Mom made three hundred little kugels using cupcake molds. She socked them away in the freezer months ahead of time. What she didn't know was that I was slowly eating them, frozen, placing other packages in front of her stash to hide my larceny. Three weeks before the big day, she went to count them. There were fifty left.

Undoubtedly a significant reason for my lifelong struggle with weight is the Jewish tradition of stuffing Jewish foods into Jewish children. This obsession with food can be traced back to Russia, where most Ashkenazi Jews like my grandparents grew up in poor villages in the Pale of Settlement. In those days of the late nineteenth and early twentieth centuries, families that had one chicken and some boiled potatoes on Shabbes considered themselves fortunate. When the immigrants arrived on these shores, the bounty of America was overwhelming. Our family business was fruits and vegetables and groceries and booze, so our dinner tables were laden with food, our pantries filled to overflowing, Bubbie cooking up a storm and instructing, "Eat! Eat!" Our family meals were never over until many of us surrendered with a bloated, "I'm stuffed!"

Fast-forward to 1993. After a lifetime of overeating, I weighed nearly three hundred pounds. I concocted a personalized diet that began on January 1 of that year. Within six months, I lost one hundred pounds! As soon as I share this story, people don't want to hear anything about my childhood, Jewish education, synagogue life, or the future of the Jewish community.

No. All they want to know is: *how did I lose 100 pounds?* Simple: I gave up all Jewish foods. I call them "K-rations"—Jewish foods that begin with the letter "k":

Kugel: Jewish noodle pudding.

Kreplach: Jewish ravioli.

Knaidel: Jewish dumplings, otherwise known as matzah balls.*

---

* "Knaidel" was the official spelling of the 2013 Scripps National Spelling Bee winning word, spelled correctly by Arvind Mahankali, a thirteen-year-old American of Indian descent.

Knish: A Jewish hot pocket.

Kasha: A very smelly grain, usually served with bow-tie pasta called *varnishkes.*

Kichel: A cookie made of sugar and air.

Knockwurst: A large hot dog.

Kippers: A little fish.

Kishke: Called "stuffed derma" on deli menus in New York City, originally intestine linings with stuffing—a long brown sausage-like concoction. (Mom and Dad bought us a dog for Hanukkah one year. It was a dachshund. I named it Kishke.)*

The one Jewish food I will never give up does not begin with the letter "k." It was one of Bubbie's specialties: *gribenes.* How do I possibly explain *gribenes?*

Let's begin with an important fact of keeping a kosher home: you cannot mix milk products with meat. This presents a huge problem for kosher cooks like Bubbie and her generation, who had no dairy-free alternatives to milk, butter, or cream. So what to do? The solution: take a pile of chicken skins, slice 'em up, and render the fat. The resulting fat is known by the most fantastic Yiddish word—*schmaltz.* Just say it; it sticks to the top of your mouth. *Schmaltz* is pure, unadulterated chicken fat that Bubbie put in her mashed potatoes instead of butter, in chopped liver, in just about everything. On Passover Zaydie lathered the stuff right onto a *schtickle* (little piece) of matzah, added salt, and presto—a terrific treat. No question, *schmaltz* is delicious. What it did to my cholesterol, I don't want to know.

After the *schmaltz* was rendered, Bubbie took the leftover shriveled chicken skins and fried them up with onions. This is

---

* I once asked an audience in Miami Beach if they could list Jewish foods beginning with the letter "k." After working through the above-mentioned list, one wise guy shouted, "Cake!"

gribenes. It's Jewish chitlins, kosher cracklins—by far, the most spec-
tacularly delicious Jewish food ever. Bubbie kept hers in a large
colander on the kitchen counter. We ate it by the handful, like
popcorn. Today you can order it at the Second Avenue Deli (which
is no longer on Second Avenue) and at Sammy's Romanian in New
York City, where there is a container of *schmaltz* on every table in a
syrup pitcher like those at IHOP. It's even making a comeback in
fancy restaurants favored by hipsters in New York City. Alana Newhouse, editor in chief of *Tablet Magazine,* holds an annual *schmaltz-*
making party that she calls a "schmixer." She and her other friends
in their twenties and thirties find the *schmaltz* to be delicious, but
the real treat are the *gribenes,* which they pair with slivovitz, the
plum brandy common to Eastern Europe. "There's nothing quite
like a slivovitz-*gribenes* high," she said. "It turns out our ancestors
were quite wise."*

Since I lost the hundred pounds, I look like a totally different
person. In fact some people think I look like a famous celebrity,
a comedian and an Academy Award–winning actor. I don't see it,
but often I am stared at or even stopped by folks who think I am
this guy. Once, in the Nate 'n Al Delicatessen in Beverly Hills, a
tourist asked me for an autograph. People walk by me on an airplane and murmur, "Look, it's Robin Williams." I never met Mr.
Williams before his tragic and untimely death, although I would
have loved to. I think he would have gotten a kick out of seeing
how much we looked alike.

Robin Williams says one of my favorite lines ever in a movie. It
is in his wonderful film *Mrs. Doubtfire.* Williams plays a divorcé who
wants to be close to his young children, so he decides to become
their nanny. He tries on a number of disguises as a female, ulti-
mately deciding on a proper Englishwoman, "Mrs. Doubtfire." But
the first disguise he puts on is of an old Jewish *bubbie.* He hunches
over, pulls on a babushka scarf, and clearly starts improvising dia-
logue. I saw this film for the first time in a movie theater in Omaha

---

* Alana Newhouse, "Schmaltz Finds a New, Younger Audience," *New York Times,*
December 9, 2014.

(Jewish population: five thousand), and when Robin Williams utters the line in the film, I was on the floor laughing hysterically. Nobody else in the theater was laughing—not even a chuckle; it went right over their heads. Here's what Robin Williams as a Jewish *bubbie* says in *Mrs. Doubtfire* (if you don't believe me, check it out on Netflix): "Never buy *gribenes* from a *moyel*."* He pauses a beat, then continues, "They're so chewy!"

One of the funniest lines in movie history—and really, really, *really* good advice.**

Gribenes

---

* *Moyel* is the Yiddish word for a ritual circumciser, the person who slices off the foreskin of an eight-day-old Jewish baby boy during the *bris* (or *brit*) *milah* (circumcision).

** If you're not Jewish, tell this true story (all my stories are true) to a Jewish friend; it's a surefire belly laugh.

Zaydie's Seder Surprise

Gribenes was the gastronomic star of our Passover Seders, the biggest holiday tradition in our extended family. Bubbie pulled out the stops for this most important family gathering of the year, working for days to make homemade gefilte fish out of the fresh carp she bought from Joe Tess the fishmonger ("Let me try *dat von*," she would tell Joe; as he picked out a live fish and held it up, Bubbie put her hand under the fish's belly and would say, "Feh, too skinny ... give me *dat von!*"), chopped liver, matzah ball soup, stuffed veal breast, carrot tzimmes, vegetables, mashed potatoes with *schmaltz*, and *Pesachdike* (kosher for Passover) cakes. Oh, the smells of her kitchen warmed your heart and your stomach, even before you took a single bite.

I knew the evening was special because we got dressed up as if going to the synagogue—Dad in a suit and tie, Mom in a lovely dress, we three boys in white shirts and slacks. This was odd to me; we never wore fancy clothes to visit Bubbie and Zaydie's house—except Seder night.

With some nineteen family members and assorted guests (up to thirty-five people), it was impossible to seat everyone in that small dining room. So tables and chairs were rented and set up in the long living room for the adults; the "kids' table" was on the sunporch.

Seder began when Zaydie sat down in his big throne-like chair at the head of the table. We picked up our Haggadahs—from Maxwell House, of course. What would you expect from a family in the grocery business?

The Maxwell House Haggadah is one of the greatest marketing successes of the twentieth century. One good thing about it: it's free! When an archeologist in the far-distant future excavates a Jewish home in, say, Teaneck, New Jersey, looking for artifacts that reveal what kind of Jews lived in the United States of America in the twentieth century, they will discover a Maxwell House Haggadah, which, on the final page of the sacred text, has *an ad for coffee!* Imagine if the famous Israeli archeologist Yigal Yadin, when he discovered the Dead Sea Scrolls in the caves of Qumran, unrolled a parchment of the ancient Torah and, on the last panel, there was an advertisement for "Shlomo's Dates." What would you think of the Essenes then?

We were like most families—reading one paragraph at a time, each adult taking a turn around the table. This lasted about ten minutes, until the relatives began asking their own version of the Four Questions upon being asked to read:

Aunt Sylvia: "What page are we on?"

Aunt Rose: "Where are my glasses?"

Aunt Ruth: "Do I *have* to read?"

Uncle Ben: "Did you see what happened in the stock market today?"

Then, every year, Uncle Mort would ask the famous "Fifth Question" of the Seder: "When do we eat?"

At that point, Zaydie would call to Bubbie—who, by the way, never set a place for herself at the table, since she was in the kitchen virtually the whole night—"Ida, bring the food!" This happened maybe fifteen minutes into the ceremony.

I always knew it was time for the meal because the men would take off their jackets and loosen their ties. Out came the gefilte fish with the slice of boiled carrot on the top, and then the soup with huge, fluffy matzah balls, followed in quick succession by all the other dishes.

Sometime between the fish and the soup, Zaydie would quietly get up and disappear. If we tried to follow him, he would shoo us back to the table. We knew what he was up to. As soon as we ate "just two more bites" of brisket, we could look for the prized *afikoman*—the final piece of matzah to be eaten at the Seder. The signal given, we madly dashed around the house, darting from lampshade to pillow cushion, frantically searching for the napkin he wrapped it in. Zaydie was a great *afikoman* hider, so we'd come running back to him, begging for clues. He loved that, taking great satisfaction from hiding the treasure so well. Finally one of us would find it, rushing back into the dining room screaming, "I found it!" to the claps and cheers of parents, aunts, and uncles, and the disappointed silence of the other cousins. My cousin Paul *never* found the *afikoman*; he was in therapy about it for years.

Presenting the broken piece of matzah to Zaydie, the finder was always first in the annual lineup of grandchildren to receive the long-awaited *afikoman* prize. Zaydie was an equal-opportunity, everybody-gets-a-present kind of Zaydie, and this was the crowning moment of the evening for him—his Passover surprise. One year he had the bookkeeper at the store go to the bank to withdraw money and place it into nine envelopes, each one inscribed with the name of one of his beloved grandchildren. Zaydie would pull them out of the front pocket of his suit, struggle to read the name, and announce the recipient of the envelope. One by one, his nine grandchildren—Nancy, Paulie, Brucie, Stevie, Billy, Ronnie, Laurie, Bobby, and Dougie—took our presents from him, whereupon he planted one of those big, wet, scratchy Zaydie kisses on our lips. This was his *naches*, his joy: the wet kisses and giving us those envelopes, each holding a brand-new, crisp, you-can-still-smell-the-ink twenty-dollar bill—a heck of a lot of money in 1958!

During dessert each of us grandchildren was coaxed into performing. This was a regular ritual at Bubbie and Zaydie's, a kind of family talent show whenever we would gather, not just at Passover, but on Friday nights after dinner and on Sunday nights after watching *The Ed Sullivan Show* on Zaydie's big-screen television. This was the opportunity for the four Paperny daughters to show off their kids and their latest tricks. Brucie Friedlander did his Elvis imitation, Stevie Luttbeg did his magic, and "Ronnie Baby," as I was nicknamed by my older cousins, sang a Pat Boone song, "April Love."

This was the beginning of my performance career, on the makeshift stage in front of Zaydie's red velvet chair with its cigarette-burn-hole arms.

Once the talent show was over, we kids ran back downstairs to the basement for general roughhousing[*] while the adults enjoyed dessert and telling stories upstairs. By now Zaydie had gone to bed, and Bubbie was just sitting down to eat something, but not before she had packed up four bundles of leftovers for each family to take home. She too would give each of us a big, wet, scratchy kiss (the hair from her mole was never plucked), and we'd take off, my brothers and I blissfully falling asleep by the time we got home.

---

[*] Cousin Laurie bore the brunt of our invented game "War." More than a few evenings ended with Laurie in a car, bleeding, on her way to the emergency room. In fact, today when I see Laurie, I often point out her scars: "See this one on her forehead? Passover 1958. See this one under her chin? Passover 1961."

A Tale of Two Bar Mitzvahs

It was the summer of 1962. The preparations for my upcoming Bar Mitzvah were in full swing. Mom was baking her cupcake-sized kugels and planning the big Saturday night party. Dad was working overtime at Louis Market, perhaps, although I don't know for sure, to take home a few extra dollars to pay for it all. As for me, I was logging a lot of time with Mr. Katz, who taught me that my real Hebrew name was not Sheket, but rather Gershon.

Mr. Katz was more than the teacher of Bar Mitzvah boys and Bat Mitzvah girls at Beth El Synagogue; he was the organizer of the daily minyan (prayer service), the chief Torah reader, the leader of services in the homes of the bereaved during the shiva week, and one of the sweetest, most beloved people on the staff of the congregation. Even though he was not formally a rabbi, he could chant the Torah by heart and knew the Talmud backwards and forwards. In the old days, he would have been called the "sexton" of the synagogue, and today he might hold the title "ritual director"; at Beth El, he was known as Reverend Alexander Katz, the only Jewish "reverend" I've ever known.

Bar/Bat Mitzvah kids were judged on their ability to lead the Shabbat morning service and by how much of the weekly Torah portion—the *sedra*—they could chant. Everybody could lead the *Sh'ma* and *v'ahavta*, recite the *Kiddush*, and chant most or all of the weekly haftarah reading and the *Maftir*, the few lines of Torah at the end of the *sedra*. A smaller number of kids could sing the *Musaf* (additional) prayers. But only the elite Bar/Bat Mitzvah students could do it all—lead the service from beginning to end and chant every single line of the often long Torah readings. This latter achievement took weeks of study and practice, since there are no vowels or musical notation in the Torah scroll itself.

Mr. Katz had an eye for the kids who had potential to become one of these do-it-all Bar Mitzvah boys. He was thrilled when my group of buddies and I showed up to learn to *layn* (chant). We all had parents who hoped we would reach the elite status, having schlepped us to junior congregation and junior choir practice nearly every week for years. As unmotivated as I was in Hebrew school, I loved performing (thanks, Ed Sullivan), and the Bar Mitzvah would be the ultimate performance in front of my adoring family and a crowded sanctuary.

An October baby, I was the youngest of our gang, the last Bar Mitzvah of the class. My Bar Mitzvah was scheduled for Shabbat Shuvah, the Sabbath between Rosh Hashanah and Yom Kippur, falling at the very beginning of the program year in the congregation. It was to be the first Bar Mitzvah in the newly renovated sanctuary at Beth El; the entire prior year, all the Bar/Bat Mitzvah services had been held in the basement social hall while the main worship space was completely overhauled. This, of course, added to the pressure to do well.

So after having mastered the designated haftarah and three lines of the *Maftir* Torah reading, I spent that summer tackling the task of learning the entire fifty-two sentences of the Torah portion *Ha'azinu*. I met with Mr. Katz weekly to review and practice the reading, and by late August he called my mother to report that I was ready to do it all, to join the elite group of boys who had also done it all. Everything was set—I knew my stuff, Mom had planned the perfect party, new clothes were bought for the occasion, and we entered the New Year with high anticipation.

And then, on the second day of Rosh Hashanah, disaster struck. In the small parking lot adjacent to the synagogue, Zaydie Louie took it upon himself to direct traffic. There were dozens of cars trying to negotiate the narrow driveway, and things quickly degenerated into chaos. Zaydie grew frustrated, his blood pressure shot up, and he collapsed in a heap. Someone called an ambulance, and he was rushed to Clarkson Hospital, where the diagnosis was swift. My beloved Zaydie had suffered a massive heart attack.

This is a good opportunity to describe what happened in my family when someone was hospitalized. Everyone moved in to the hospital. Literally. The *gantze mishpoche* (whole family). The waiting room on the patient floor was commandeered, food was brought in, and a steady stream of visitors came to comfort those enduring the vigil. At least three of the four daughters were in Zaydie's room at all times, and they each took turns sleeping overnight on a recliner by his bedside. Someone needed to be there, not just to tend to Zaydie, but to interrogate the doctors, to await the test results, to supervise the nurses. For his part, Zaydie, who recovered nicely, *schmeered* (bribed) the nurses to sneak him cigarettes.

Although it was frowned upon by the religious authorities to postpone a *simcha* (celebration) for almost any reason in order not to undermine the life-cycle moment, there was no way I was to become a Bar Mitzvah without Zaydie present. No way. Certainly my mother could not imagine it, and neither could I. He was my everything, my hero. No, the Bar Mitzvah would have to be postponed until Zaydie could be there.

And so that next Shabbat morning, as originally planned, I chanted the Torah portion I had so studiously prepared all summer, simply to not let all that effort go for naught. On the very next day, I met with Mr. Katz to begin to learn *another* Torah portion for the rescheduled Bar Mitzvah in December. By then Zaydie was healthy and back at work, and he proudly took his place in the front row of the congregation. He cried tears of joy as I led the packed house in the greatest performance of my life, including chanting the entire second Torah reading. At the party that night in the social hall of the synagogue, after the miniature hot dog hors d'oeuvres, the champagne fountain drinks, and Mom's cupcake kugels were consumed, Zaydie gave the toast: "Ronnie, I am proud of you, like I'm proud of all my grandchildren. You've given me *naches*. I love you."

And I loved him. Oh, did I love him ...

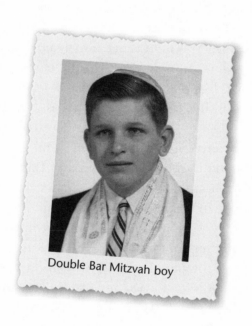

Double Bar Mitzvah boy

Missing Shabbes

After my Bar Mitzvah, I did what most kids did—I quit Hebrew school and I stopped showing up at the synagogue. As an Israeli friend of mine who tutors Bar and Bat Mitzvah kids likes to say after each kid performs, "You want to see him again? Take a picture."

I entered what can only be called the early adolescent rebellion stage of life. It was a rebellion not just against our extended family's traditions, but against my parents as well. My mother was the only one of Zaydie and Bubbie's four daughters who kept Jewish tradition alive in her own home. On a daily basis there was Yiddish spoken in the house; Mom and Dad both grew up in Yiddish-speaking homes, so they spoke it to each other as a kind of secret language in the presence of us boys if they didn't want us to know what they were talking about. Mom insisted on keeping kosher so her mother could eat there. Oh, we ate *treif* (nonkosher food) when we went out; Dad's favorite food was a tenderloin sandwich—tenderloin as in *pork* tenderloin! He went along with the Jewish stuff to appease Mom. Truth is, he rebelled against his father's Jewish Orthodoxy when a teenager; talked to me about his great Jewish hero, Spinoza, the famous Jewish atheist; and shared his own doubts about the existence of God.

Mom always insisted on Shabbat dinner together. Even though she was very busy raising three boys and running her own advertising business, Friday night was sacred time in our house—a tradition. She lit Shabbat candles, just like her mother did. All four of us men were expected to be at the table at six o'clock sharp.

One Friday afternoon I was hanging out with friends at the local shopping mall, having a great time, until I looked at my watch. It read seven-thirty. I hopped on the bus and strolled into the house at eight. The Shabbat candles were lit, dinner had been eaten, and Mom was on the phone with the police, crying, worried that I had been in an accident or shot. I knew I was in trouble, but I had no idea I was about to learn one of the most important lessons of my life.

Dad saw me walk in, embraced me with a sigh of relief, and then turned angry: "Ronnie, where have you been! You missed Shabbes dinner!"

I replied, as only an adolescent could, "So what, Dad? You don't believe in any of this religious stuff anyway!"

Now I can't exactly remember what happened next. But when things calmed down, Dad and I had one of those father-son talks that will stay with me forever.

"I am so disappointed in you, Ronnie," he began. "Your mother was frantic. We had no idea where you were, if you were in trouble. It's a terrible feeling. You know that we expect you to be at the dinner table on Friday night!"

"I'm sorry, Dad," I mumbled. "I should have called you; I didn't realize what time it was. But I still don't get why it's so important to be home Friday night. You tell me you don't believe in God!"

Dad hesitated a moment and then spilled his heart out to me: "You wanna know why? I'll tell you why. I work like a dog every day, all week long. I take off one night a week—Friday night. Your uncles don't like it—you wanna know why? Friday night is the busiest night of the week in the grocery business—you wanna know why? I'll tell you why—people get their paychecks on Friday, and the first thing they do is buy food and booze. I'll tell you something else; our friends don't like it, either—you wanna know why? I'll tell you why—Saturday night is a big social night in Omaha, and they want us to go with them out on the town—but your mother and I never go out Saturday night. 'Cause I'm working every Saturday night, so I can take off Friday night. You wanna know why?"

"Yeah, Dad, why?"

"So I can be with your mother and my boys for a meal, a meal that isn't rushed, a meal that's taken at the dining room table, not in front of the TV, a meal where I can sit and talk with you about school and your week. Then I kick off my shoes, and we play a game or read a book. You wanna know why it's so important to be home Friday night? Because it's our *family* time—it's the best time of my week. That's why!"

As Dad said the words "it's our family time," his voice began to soften, to choke up. I looked into my father's eyes as they reddened. And then, for the first time in my life, my dad cried in front of me.

I never missed another Shabbat dinner—to this day.

Never Underestimate
Your Mother

I was terrible at being an adolescent—pudgy, not especially handsome, and once I abandoned my Hebrew school buddies, I was lost socially. Just about anything my parents wanted me to do, I didn't, especially if it involved going to synagogue. My parents were frantic; they had moved to a house six blocks from the shul so my brothers and I could easily walk there, but I wanted nothing to do with it. They tried everything to get me to go back. No way.

The summer before ninth grade, flyers started to appear in the mail from the local chapter of the youth group at Beth El Synagogue, BILU United Synagogue Youth (USY). I ignored them. This drove my mother nuts; I was hanging out with some of the wilder kids at Lewis and Clark junior high school, trying to be cool. It didn't work; I wasn't hip enough or rich enough to make it with the in crowd. So as Bubbie would have said, I was *nisht a hin, nisht a hare*, "neither here nor there." The Beatles, who were about to invade the United States of America, would have called me a "Nowhere Man"; I had no group of friends, and frankly, I was floundering.

One Sunday afternoon in August 1963, my mother came into my bedroom holding a flyer inviting me to a new-member barbecue at the synagogue youth lounge. "Why don't you go up there, Ronnie?" she suggested as she handed me the flyer. "They're having hot dogs, hamburgers ... give it a try." I took the flyer, crumpled it up and threw it back at her, muttering, "I'm not going."

Mom was completely fed up. "Okay, fine. Your father and I are going out for dinner—you are on your own, son!" and she huffed out of the room.

A couple of hours later I began to get the growlies and went into the kitchen searching for something to eat. When I flung open the refrigerator, there was nothing in it except a bottle of Heinz ketchup.

Mom, God love her, had completely emptied it. I don't know what she did with the food, but it wasn't there. I couldn't believe it! I slammed shut the refrigerator in disgust ... and what do I see? Smoothed out and pasted on the front door of that fridge? The flyer from USY offering free food! I muttered to myself, "Ooooooh, my mother!"

I had no choice; I was famished. So I reluctantly walked up to the "gogue" as we called it, strolled into the youth lounge—and there were all my buddies, my old friends from Hebrew school. They greeted me warmly: "Hey, Ronnie, welcome back!" "Hey, Ronnie, where you been?" "Hey, Ronnie, did you ever get the spit out of your face?"

They were having a great time. As I looked around, I noticed the boys had not gone through puberty, but the girls had—most definitely. Then this really cool young guy, Jack Molad, the new youth director, got up and with an enthusiasm that took my breath away, announced all the great things we were going to do in USY, including an all-night bus ride to St. Louis for the regional convention over Thanksgiving weekend. I thought to myself, "Hmmm. All night on a bus with those girls ... sounds great to me! Sign me up!"

I was hooked; I had found my group. I took to USY like a duck takes to water. I went to everything with my buddies; we called ourselves "the Bunch." I got on the fast track to becoming a *macher* (big shot) in USY. I was recruited to be the chapter regalia chairman (I was in charge of pins) in my freshman year, elected chapter vice president in my sophomore year, elected chapter president and second vice president of EMTZA (Midwest; literally, "middle") Region USY in my junior year. On a train ride from Minneapolis to

Chicago for the International USY Convention in December 1965, a fellow board member, Ellen Kushner, and I wrote a new regional song to the tune of the Gillette razor blade commercial, a song still sung today, a song that will perhaps be my longest-lasting legacy in Jewish life:

> We're EMTZA and we're on the ball,
> We're the region that did start it all,
> So stand up and give a great big cheer
> For EMTZA Region now is here!

In my senior year I ran for and won the office of regional president of EMTZA Region USY, a territory spanning the Midwest from Winnipeg, Canada, in the north to St. Louis in the south, Iowa City in the east, and Denver in the west. I spent seventeen weekends of that year on the road, traveling to a different city and synagogue each time to meet with the local teenagers and, sometimes, speak to the congregation about living Jewishly.

I've been on the road doing pretty much the same thing ever since, telling my true stories.

Tevye

In the summer of 1966 EMTZA USY held a ten-day summer encampment at Esther K. Newman, a camp just outside of Omaha. On the first day we were introduced to the staff, including a drama counselor from New York City who had been recruited to do a musical theater workshop. He had a vinyl LP of the original cast album and a copy of the recently published Dell paperback "book" of the hottest musical on Broadway, a show with "Jewish themes"—*Fiddler on the Roof*. The musical had only opened on September 22, 1964, and won nine Tony Awards, including for best musical, in 1965. Very few people in Nebraska or the Midwest had seen the show; it was nearly impossible to get a ticket. Certainly none of us teenagers had seen it or knew the music.

On day one someone typed up and mimeographed scripts, and we listened to the recording of the Broadway songs. On day two we auditioned for parts. (Earlier that spring I had played Alfred P. Doolittle in Central High's production of *My Fair Lady*.) I was cast as Tevye: "A fiddler on the roof! Sounds crazy, no? But, in our little village of Anatevka, one thing helps us keep our balance. Tradition!"

Frankly I have no idea how we managed to learn our parts in such a short span of time. But we loved it. After all, we were teenagers in a synagogue youth movement, trying to figure out what it meant to be a young Jew in 1966. We were living the Shabbat of "Sunrise, Sunset." Many of our grandparents came to the United States from Russian villages like Anatevka. We could relate to the

36

challenges of adolescent rebellion and the tension between tradition and change.

So on the tenth night of USY summer camp in August 1966, our little troupe of performers took to a makeshift stage in the basement of the dining room at Camp Esther K. Newman in front of a room packed with fellow campers and some of the parents and family members of the Omaha cast members, including my parents and brothers. Our costumes were rudimentary. The sets and props were sparse. But from the opening note to the final curtain, the audience sat transfixed as we put on a pretty good performance of *Fiddler*. There were laughs, there were tears, and there was a thunderous standing ovation as we took our curtain calls. Wonder of wonder, miracles of miracles, indeed!

The summer camp show was such a success and so many of the key parts were played by Omaha kids, someone thought it would be a great idea to do the show again for the members of Beth El Synagogue. Moreover, the annual EMTZA Regional Convention was to be hosted at a hotel in Omaha over Thanksgiving weekend, just three months later. Why not do the show on the opening night of the convention for the five hundred teenagers expected to attend? So new kids were recruited to take roles—my brother Bobby played Lazar Wolf the Butcher—better costumes and sets were created, and once again *Fiddler on the Roof* was performed three more times in Nebraska—to standing-room-only audiences at the convention and in the social hall at Beth El. The synagogue called the performances "A Night of Jewish Music," but I never understood why. The response to the show was overwhelming. It turns out, we kids were quite talented performers, even if the audience mostly consisted of family members and friends. Can you imagine the *naches* of my parents and brothers, my *bubbie* and *zaydie*, and my aunts, uncles, and cousins watching "Ronnie Baby" belt out "If I Were A Rich Man"? Those nights I really did feel like the best boy in the United States of America.

Recently, I told a New York City–based theater director the story of my four performances in *Fiddler*.

"You know why the synagogue called the performance 'A Night of Jewish Music'?" he mused. "It was totally illegal! In 1966 there were no licensing rights for high schools to do a production of *Fiddler*. But do you realize, Ron, you were probably the first person *ever* to play Tevye outside of Broadway?"

I asked Alisa Solomon, author of *Wonder of Wonders: A Cultural History of Fiddler on the Roof*, if that could possibly be true. Her answer: by August 1966 there was a national tour company and an Israeli production of *Fiddler*. "But, no doubt," she concluded, "you, Ron, were the first amateur ever to play Tevye!"

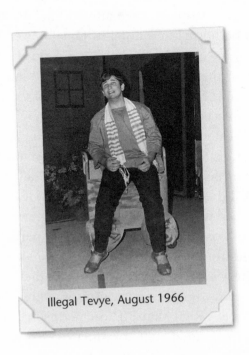

Illegal Tevye, August 1966

Mom

Tradition. Tradition. Papas. Mamas. These were the ingredients of my *geshmak* (tasty) family. Little did I realize at the time that the traditions of my *zaydie* and *bubbie*, our extended family, and my mom and dad would profoundly shape my worldview and my identity as a second-generation American Jew, growing up in "our little village" of Omaha, Nebraska.

My mother, Bernice, was an extraordinary woman, even though, coming after three sisters, she was meant to be a boy. Smart, clever, and ambitious, she was the only one of the four Paperny girls with aspirations to be in business. Bernice was treated like a son by her father, Louie, who taught her his business from the time she could talk. Zaydie would take his Bernice downtown to the produce market to buy from Greenberg Fruit and other wholesalers. He taught her how to compute complicated mathematical formulas in her head, just like he did. Louie, a man with no formal education, could figure out how much he needed to charge for a pound of bananas simply by knowing the wholesale price and the size of the load—without the use of a calculator. He also taught her a love for retail business—the hustle and bustle of customers, products, deals, fast cash. I've often said that my mother did not have a good day unless it concluded with counting money from a cash register.

Louie was an excellent teacher; Bernice turned out to be a very successful businesswoman at a time when most women were stay-at-home moms. She graduated from the University of Nebraska–Lincoln (Johnny Carson was in her class) with a degree in journalism. As soon as her three boys were all safely ensconced in full-day elementary school, she started her own advertising business. She did the weekly ad for Louis Market and for Goldstein-Chapman, a women's clothing store downtown. By the time of my Bar Mitzvah, she was restless and decided to open a retail business.

Mom applied for a Mr. Donut franchise. She had the perfect location, on a busy corner across from Benson High School, not three blocks from Louis Market, and my Bar Mitzvah money as a down payment. But the East Coast Mr. Donut people would not award a franchise to a woman. So, typical of Mom, she thought, "Screw you, I'll create my own donut shop." She transformed the building into a Swiss chalet with red flocked wallpaper, wrought-iron-backed chairs with red leather seats, and mahogany counters. She had an artist design a cartoon character, a little Swiss man in lederhosen, who held a distinctive coffee cup. She researched the best flours and ingredients to make spectacular donuts. While other cake donuts had a smear of icing on top, Mom invented a device to completely immerse the donuts in thick white or chocolate icing and then added nuts, coconut, or sprinkles, so the entire donut was covered in toppings. She brewed the best coffee in town and offered endless free refills. She gave free coffee and donuts to the local police, who frequented the twenty-four-hour business often, especially during the night shift, so she never worried about security—such a smart *Yiddishe kup* (head/mind)! Mom wanted her customers to see the donuts being made, so she installed a round window on the wall separating the bakery from the counters. Around the window, she had an artist create a cake donut on which was written the following saying:

As you ramble on through life, brother,
Whatever be your goal;
Keep your eye upon the donut
And not upon the hole!

It was a magical recipe for business success. On the first day the shop opened, she ran out of donuts, dissolving in tears. The next day the baker doubled the dozens, and she was off and running. Mom built her Dippy Donut Shoppes into a chain of twelve stores throughout Nebraska. In fact Mr. Donut decided not to come to Omaha after all; they couldn't compete with Bernice. Oh, and I got to learn how to fry donuts. In vegetable oil. No lard in Bernice Wolfson's donut shoppe.

This success led to Mom's next venture, The Deli at Westroads, a Jewish delicatessen (the first in Omaha—"I'll have the pastrami on one of them bah-gels!" her mostly non-Jewish customers would say). She refused to serve dairy products and shipped in kosher deli meats from Chicago. But within two months, she gave in to the demands of her customers who wanted a glass of milk with their corned beef sandwich. The Deli was a big hit in the largest shopping center in the state.

When a space became available next to The Deli, Mom went into the bar business. She decorated the place with antique back bars and installed an old revolving door at the entrance, hence the name of the place, The Revolving Door Lounge. After I saw it in a club in Burbank, California, Mom brought karaoke to Omaha, and the lounge took off.

After many years in the food business, Mom's last business venture was a consignment clothing store for plus-sized women called "Babes."*

Beyond her businesses, Mom devoted most of her time to family and helping others. She adored her three older sisters— four girls who grew up literally in the same room together, as close as four human beings can be. You would think that with four sisters there would be envy, jealousy, and jockeying for position in the family. But if there was one value that Bubbie and Zaydie instilled in their girls it was this: *one for all and all for one.* They were taught to

---

* That's what Dad called Mom—"Babe"—a term of endearment among men of a certain age. His license plate for years read "Babes." Most people thought he owned a strip club.

enjoy each other's achievements and successes and to be there for each other when times were tough. Years later when I had children of my own, I thought back to that crucial value. There is a natural competitiveness among siblings, but when the message sent from the parents is "family is more important than anything," children learn that there is a greater good beyond the self.

This centrality of family leads to something else—extraordinary loyalty. The Paperny girls were totally devoted to their parents, idolizing Zaydie and doting on Bubbie. They shared every detail of their lives with each other, talking with each other at least once, sometimes several times a day, telling funny or exaggerated stories about their kids or grandkids. "Did you hear about so-and-so? He just started a new job and he's already the CEO!" Years later, we called this "the BubbieNet." Oh, they would argue, and they would call each other out when they thought someone was wrong. But in the end, there was always reconciliation and forgiveness, born out of a deep love for each other. No matter what, family trumps all.

And beyond family, Mom believed in the value of community. She loved Beth El Synagogue, the sacred community her parents had helped establish. For twenty-five years, every Friday night, she sang in the volunteer choir at shul. We rushed through dinner so Mom could get to the synagogue to rehearse with Cantor Aaron I. Edgar.

One day in 1958 a friend at the synagogue, Pauline Guss, told Mom about a national sisterhood conference she had just returned from. "Bernice, you wouldn't believe it! There was a young Jewish blind boy, Sparky Mandel, who thanked a local congregational sisterhood for help in transcribing a Braille prayer book so he could have a Bar Mitzvah. Do you think we could start a Braille group at Beth El?"

This tap on the shoulder inspired Mom. "I don't see why not," she said to Pauline. "Let me call Rabbi Kripke to see what we can do."

Rabbi Kripke was enthusiastic about the idea and offered a small room in the basement. Mom recruited some girlfriends to join her, they taught each other how to transcribe Braille, they raised money for duplicating equipment, and it was done. The Braille Group's first project was the first English-Hebrew Passover Haggadah in Braille.

Mom was transformed as she pursued her very own repair-the-world project. There were no Jewish blind children in Omaha, but there were plenty of blind kids, most of whom were being sent to a terrible asylum in nearby Nebraska City. Mom learned that there were eight blind kids in Omaha who needed a preschool, but no institution would host them. She knew that the synagogue preschool met on Monday, Wednesday, and Friday mornings, so she called her rabbi again.

"Rabbi, do you think I could borrow the preschool equipment on Tuesdays and Thursdays so we can run a nursery school for the blind kids?"

"Absolutely," Rabbi Kripke agreed. Another girlfriend, Ruth Sokoloff, volunteered to head up the preschool.

Mom then thought the kids would benefit from a summer camp experience, so she arranged to have the older blind kids come to the local Salvation Army summer camp for a week. She took Gene Eppley, the richest man in Omaha at the time (Eppley Airfield is named for him), out to see the kids having a fantastic time and asked him for support. The next day Eppley called her to offer $10,000—a large sum of money then.

"But Bernice," he cautioned, "you'll have to create a 501c3 nonprofit corporation for me to make the donation."

Overnight Mom established the Nebraska Foundation for Visually Impaired Children to gather funding and support, recruiting a board that included ophthalmologists, social workers, donors, and blind activists. She thought the kids should have an annual Christmas party, so she recruited Ruth Sokoloff's husband, Phil, a prominent businessman, to sponsor the event. The blind children got twenty-five dollars each and a sighted helper to go shopping for Christmas presents for their parents and siblings.

Honestly, I don't know how she did it. She was raising three rambunctious boys, running her own businesses, volunteering at the synagogue, making daily visits to her elderly parents—and yet she found time to throw herself into working on behalf of the blind kids and their families. Her efforts were widely lauded; one of the proudest days of my life was when this busy mom was honored as the Omaha "Volunteer of the Year" in 1961. I even got to leave school early to attend the luncheon!

Through her work as chairwoman of the foundation, Mom met a number of famous blind personalities when they came through Omaha. One year the outstanding blind jazz pianist George Shearing played a weeklong engagement in town during Passover. Mom met him at an event and invited him to our home for Seder on the second night of the holiday. I will never forget the excitement of having a famous personality in our home! Shearing was delightful, participating fully in the Seder ceremony and reading from the Braille Haggadah my mother had worked so hard to produce. The next evening he invited all of us to attend his concert. His assistant walked him to the piano bench; he sat down, greeted the crowd, and said, "It's been wonderful to be in Omaha this week, and last night I had the most extraordinary experience with the Wolfson family ..." and then George Shearing proceeded to play a jazz variation of *Dayenu!*

Forty years later I met George backstage after a concert. He remembered the evening as if it were yesterday: "Ronnie, how are your parents, Bernice and Alan? Ronnie, guess what? Someone helped me do my genealogy, and we discovered my grandmother was Jewish. That makes me Jewish, doesn't it, Ronnie?" I hugged him with the answer, "Why, yes it does, George!"

At the fiftieth anniversary celebration of the foundation, much to her stunned surprise, Bernice Wolfson was the honoree. She was chairman of the board from the day the foundation was created until the day she died, improving the lives of the blind children and adults in Nebraska.

This was Mom. A force of nature. She got things done. She worked the phones like a skilled politician. For her, life was a symphony, and she was the conductor—at home, at the businesses, at the foundation, and in the extended family. Even when she struggled with illness in the last few years of her life, she orchestrated dinners, celebrations, vacations, and programs—all from her everheld-to-her-ear phone near her lift recliner chair. She taught me how to honor parents. She taught me how to be an entrepreneur. She taught me loyalty. She taught me that as busy as you are, there is always time to work on *tikkun olam,* perfecting the world, to care for those beyond the Jewish community. She taught me to be creative, to be relentless in pursuing my dreams, to perform to the best of my ability. She taught me to put others first.

She was something, my mom.

Mom at The Deli

Mom holding the Braille Haggadah

Dad

This is a true story—a fish-out-of-water true story.

My father, Alan, was a Brooklyn-born gregarious soul. He also talked funny. That is, he had a pronounced Brooklyn accent. This made him quite a standout in Omaha, Nebraska. While Omahans pronounce the word "orange" as a monosyllabic "oarnge," Dad turned it into a three-syllable "ah-ren-ge." For most Omahans, a "beautiful" day is a "b'yout'full" day. For Dad, it was a "bee-you-tee-full" day. I'm surprised his customers could understand him!

Movie-star handsome and charming, Alan swept Bernice Paperny off her feet. Mom was engaged to a nice Jewish boy from Lexington, Kentucky, who she had met when attending the university there for a semester. His name was Raymond, and he bought her a diamond ring the size of a small boulder, but when he visited Omaha to meet the family, he failed to impress. Bubbie Ida took her daughter aside and administered a swift judgment in her sharp-tongued Yiddish: "*Ers nisht gut fur dir!*" ("He's not good for you!") That ended the engagement; mothers had that kind of power then.

A few months later, Louie and Ida Paperny traveled to a wedding of one of Bubbie's relatives in Brooklyn and met Celia and Isadore Wolfson, who had an unmarried son just out of the army. "Look," Louie said to Isadore, "you've got a *boychik* [boy] and we've got a *shayna maidel* [pretty girl]. Maybe they'll be a match. Send him to Omaha!"

Alan made the trip to Omaha for a New Year's Eve celebration in 1947. Bernice set up Alan with one of her girlfriends, and she brought along another guy as her date, but before the clock struck twelve, the couples had switched partners. Mom fell hard for this "gorgeous" guy from Brooklyn who could have been Ronald Reagan's stand-in, and Dad fell just as hard for his voluptuous relative. So my parents were actually third cousins. Within a year, they were married.

Fish out of water or not, Dad proved to be a hard worker. He had quit high school to go to work when his father went bust in an ill-fated business in the Catskill Mountains. Then World War II came along and he enlisted, serving at Fitzsimmons Army Hospital near Denver, Colorado. Once married to Mom, he entered the world of Louis Market with youthful enthusiasm, joining his older brothers-in-law in building the business.

Selling groceries and liquor led to long days and nights at the store, with only occasional time off—an afternoon nap here, a rare day off there. He called his boys "my three sons," and he loved to engage us. The time spent with Dad was always fueled by his boyish enthusiasm and occasional anxiety to teach us how to do things. Like bowling. Dad loved bowling, and he would schlep us to the bowling alley for lessons. Or to the golf course. Or sometimes fishing. Or swimming. Having grown up near Brighton Beach and Coney Island, Dad was a fantastic swimmer who loved demonstrating his ability to stay underwater for what seemed like hours.

Dad also loved showing off his vocabulary. Never having gone to college, he was determined to teach himself big words, mostly garnered from his voracious reading. And he loved to use them, impressing those in his orbit who were better educated. He wrote poetry and loved to make up pithy philosophical sayings— "Ronnie," he once told me, "the center of 'life' is 'if'!"

Dad was endlessly *dreying* (*drey*, as in *dreydle*, means "spinning"), a perfect characteristic for someone who aspired to be an inventor. A dental technician in World War II, he dreamed for years of inventing a new kind of toothbrush, one that would brush both sides of the teeth simultaneously. He thought it would be useful for children, the elderly, and even dogs. He played with numerous ideas, but none of them really worked. Then one day he experienced a flash of inspiration while watching a custodian polish the floor in a shopping mall. He reasoned that a circular brush, like the one on the floor polisher, would do a much better job cleaning the teeth and gums than the standard rectangular brush. By setting two small circular brushes facing each other, you could brush both sides of the teeth at the same time! He called his newfangled toothbrush "Brushrite."

To tell the truth, the first prototype of Dad's toothbrush hardly evoked "aha"s. In fact, most people who saw it reacted with "ha-ha"s. It didn't help that he crudely fashioned the two brushes on the end of a plastic water pistol, which looked pretty scary when he stuck it in his mouth to demonstrate! Honestly, we all thought his idea was a little loony. Undaunted, he applied for and was awarded a United States of America patent on the thing and took it to an inventors fair in a small Nebraska town, setting up his own booth with handwritten signs touting the benefits of his Brushrite. Wouldn't you know it? Someone saw the potential in the thing and bought the rights from Dad to manufacture a version of the toothbrush that attracted interest from a company that had taken the country by storm.

That company, Epilady, was one of the greatest marketing successes of the 1980s. Invented by the head of a South African Jewish family, the Epilady was a device that eliminated hair from women's legs. Manufactured on a kibbutz in Israel and imported to the United States, Epilady was positioned as a cosmetic appliance, sold next to perfumes and makeup in the department stores. This gave the Epilady a scent of excellence, a highbrow device for a lowbrow problem. With a multimillion-dollar marketing campaign on television and in magazines, Epilady was a must-have item in a woman's toolbox of beauty aids.

The Epilady people were looking for another product to bring to market, another personal hygiene device that could be marketed with the same élan. Wouldn't you know it? They discovered Dad's toothbrush, a unique take on a product that everyone—not just women—needed daily. Rebranding it as the "Epi-Dent Rotary Toothbrush," the company produced a television commercial and prepared a nationwide rollout.

For Dad, it was as if he had won the lottery. With a major marketing company behind the Epi-Dent, he not only felt validated, he could barely sleep, dreaming of the riches from the royalties that were undoubtedly coming his way. He was thrilled when he learned that the first store to offer the Epi-Dent was the flagship Bloomingdale's in his native New York City. I accompanied Dad and Mom to the department store on Fifty-Ninth and Lexington, where sure enough the Epi-Dent was displayed and demonstrated on the famous Bloomie's cosmetic aisle, right next to the Epilady. Dad's whole body shook, tears of joy streaming down his face as the beautiful people of New York City began to buy his invention. You would have thought he had just won the Nobel Prize.

Within a week of this penultimate moment in his life as an inventor, Dad received devastating news: the Epilady people were in trouble. Although the company had sold millions of Epilady devices, millions of them were returned. Turns out the thing was a torture instrument. It literally pulled women's leg hair out of the skin, causing enormous pain and discomfort. At the same time one of the daughters in the South African family invested four million dollars in a Broadway show that opened on Thursday and closed on Friday. The company went bankrupt ... just before the national marketing campaign for the Epi-Dent went live.

At first Dad was despondent. His dreams of solving everyone's financial problems, of making significant donations to charities like the Nebraska Foundation for Visually Impaired Children, of leaving us kids a pile of money, of maybe buying a boat, vanished into thin air. "This was to be my legacy for you, Ronnie," he cried to me.

"But, Dad," I replied, "think of what you achieved. Most inventors never get their products produced, much less bought and marketed by a major company. We are so proud of you. And Dad, your legacy is not money or fame. Your legacy is teaching us to be tenacious in the face of doubters. We all laughed at your folly, but your folly turned into something incredibly useful and important. No one's laughing at Alan Wolfson now, regardless of what happens with the toothbrush. Your legacy is giving all of us boys the inspiration to follow our dreams, just like you followed yours."

Dad's three sons did exactly that. Bobby dreamed of starring in a play, so when he was eight years old, he walked into the Omaha Community Playhouse to audition for a part in an adult production of *All the Way Home*—*without* telling Mom or Dad. He got the part and was a big hit.

Bright and quick, Bobby inherited Dad's *dreying*, always thinking, always moving. I like to say he had a severe case of *shpilkosis.** During the tumultuous late sixties and early seventies Bobby attended five universities, leading to a parody song at the rehearsal dinner before his wedding to Sibby just before Passover in 1976:

> Bobby Wolfson went to college, went to college,
> Went to college, went to college, went to college,
> *Dayenu!* (Enough!)

After law school, Bobby served as the beloved regional director of the Plains States Region of the Anti-Defamation League, based in Omaha for eighteen years, and then he was recruited to New York City by Abe Foxman to head up all twenty-seven regions of the ADL, an incredibly important position in the American Jewish community.

Brother Dougie graduated from the University of Arizona, returned to Omaha to work in the family businesses, and became a leading advocate for children and young adults with special needs. When he and his wife, Sara, realized their son Avi was born with a chromosomal condition that rendered him speechless, they refused to institutionalize him, courageously raising him in their home and mainstreaming him in the local schools.

---

* *Shpilkis:* "Can't sit still."

Just like my parents and grandparents, I am incredibly proud of my "bros." Undoubtedly, their advocacy for repairing the world is a sincere combination of Mom's model of social justice work and Dad's passion for finding solutions to life's challenges.

And what happened to Dad's ingenious toothbrush? Eventually, another company did bring Dad's invention to market as Oralgenie, sold primarily through catalogs as a children's toothbrush. Dad never got rich, but we all felt enriched by his dedication to his vision.

Left to right: Mom's date, Mom, Dad's date, Dad—before the switch

Mom and Dad and their boys

The Merchants of Omaha

Like a character in a novel, Omaha has a quiet but unforgettable personality. It's not Garrison Keillor's Lake Wobegon, but pretty darn close. It sits almost precisely in the center of the United States, on the banks of the muddy Missouri River, a small and shallow tributary that forms the eastern border of Nebraska. It's the only serious body of water in the entire state. (Well, there is Carter Lake—a pond near the airport—and when I was a kid, a swimming hole with a real sandy beach at Peony Park, an amusement place our kids, who grew up with Disneyland in their backyard, called "Teeny Weeny Park," but I'm getting ahead of myself.)

Landlocked Nebraskans have a wry, endearing self-deprecating sense of humor. When celebrities come a-visiting, they are not offered the same symbolic gestures as they get in most places—the keys to the city. No. In our water-starved state, you get an "admiralty" in the Great Navy of the State of Nebraska.

The humor continues with the name of the most important civic association of those in Omaha high society: "Ak-Sar-Ben." (Read it backwards.) When I was a kid, Ak-Sar-Ben occupied a sprawling complex of buildings in southwest Omaha, including a horse racing track and an auditorium/social hall that seated about five thousand for concerts and was transformed into a popular indoor skating rink in the winter. The society folks held an annual "Ak-Sar-Ben Coronation Ball," a fund-raiser in which the Knights of Ak-Sar-Ben anointed a prominent man and woman "king" and "queen" of the mythical "kingdom" of "Quivira." Young debutantes made their debut on the social scene in formal dress; the chosen few were named "Ak-Sar-Ben princesses," while young men dressed in military-like uniforms escorted them to the ball. To me, it was always very exclusive and silly, but it was a big deal when a Jewish businessman was named "king of Quivira," breaking through the notoriously WASPish character of Omaha's social scene.

The humor extends to the words of the most famous song in the state—the University of Nebraska Cornhuskers football fight song:

> There is no place like Nebraska,
> Dear old Nebraska U!
> Where the girls are the fairest,
> The boys are the squarest,
> Of any old school that I knew.
> There is no place like Nebraska,
> Where they're all true blue.
> We'll all stick together,
> In all kinds of weather,
> For dear old Nebraska U!

They weren't kidding about the weather. Sitting smack dab in the middle of the Great Plains of the central United States of America, there is nothing buffeting the winds sweeping into the city from the west or the cold Arctic air dipping in from the north. Winters can be brutally cold, with blizzard conditions, while May brings tornadoes and summers are humid and hot. Honestly, there are really only two times a year to visit Nebraska: the two weeks of great weather in the fall when the enormous urban forest of trees that embrace the city explodes in a riot of autumnal color, and the two weeks of mild temperatures and rebirth of the foliage from their winter slumber in the spring.

You would think Nebraska is as flat as a pancake. It is—once you get outside of the city. But Omaha is blessed with undulating hills that give the place a lovely character. It is the Missouri River that carved the hills of Omaha. Most people are shocked when they visit the city to see how really lovely it is. Some think Omaha is a bunch of farms and cows; after all, when I was a kid, the largest stockyards in the country were in downtown Omaha on Twenty-Fourth Street. On a Sunday evening, when the wind was just right, you could smell those cows as the ranchers trucked in their herds to the meat-packing district. We would sit on our porch and take in that stiff whiff of manure; some nights the odor was so strong it would force us indoors.

There was money in them thar cows. A bunch of Jewish families were in the meat-packing business. My best friend Milt Erman's dad was one. When Mr. Erman picked up Milt and me for carpool, Milt got to sit shotgun, while I was relegated to the backseat, right next to the trunk, where Mr. Erman kept the hip-high boots he wore to visit his cows. Pee-yew! I could barely breathe the whole way home. Another Jewish family, the Simons, turned corn-fed beef into a national brand, Omaha Steaks.

The most charming part of Omaha was—and is—the Old Market. A six-block area situated downtown near the Union Station, the brick buildings housed the bustling wholesale fruit and vegetable market of the growing city. The Union Pacific Railroad began in Omaha and crossed the country all the way to San Francisco—the Golden Spike marking the point where the tracks from the West Coast met the tracks from the Midwest. Today the Old Market is a big tourist attraction, the warehouses transformed into upscale eateries, art galleries, and loft apartments.

It was the railroad that attracted a large influx of immigrants to Omaha in the early twentieth century. Polish Catholics, Irish Catholics, New England Protestants, and Jewish refugees from the crowded tenements of the Lower East Side of New York and South Boston made their way west to Omaha, knowing that the railroad brought commerce. They arrived with nothing but the shirt on their backs but quickly realized you could buy fruits and vegetables from the local farmers, put them on a wagon, and peddle them to a growing population attracted to the town.

That is exactly how Zaydie Louie got his start. He peddled fruits and vegetables from a wagon until he had enough money to buy a piece of property and set up a roadside stand. But instead of buying where the Jews were, Louie purchased a lot on the Radial Highway in a neighborhood of Omaha called Benson. His friends thought he was crazy, but Louie knew the city was growing north. So he moved his wife and four girls to Benson, far away from the center of the Jewish community.

Louis Fruits and Vegetables was a huge success from the get-go, mainly because Louie Paperny was a master merchandiser with a magical formula of low prices, massive inventories, and a warm personal style. We have a panoramic photograph taken of that corner in 1932. A large open-air fruit and vegetable stand with a canopy dominates one side of the property, while a small "family bar" and package liquor store is situated on the other. (Rumor has it Zaydie sold booze during Prohibition, possibly through connections with Al Capone in Chicago, and there were reportedly piles of cash under the basement stairs.) There are large bushels of melons with signs reading "Special: 50 cents" and 25-cent baskets of homegrown tomatoes standing along the curb, beckoning customers to come in for the bargains. It is difficult to identify all the store employees standing erect for the photo, dressed in shirtsleeves and white aprons. But just inside the overhang of the canopy, I can make out Zaydie Louie, a short, stocky man. Standing right next to him is a little girl—my mother, Bernice. On top of the building is a simple word: "Louis," which everyone in Omaha pronounced

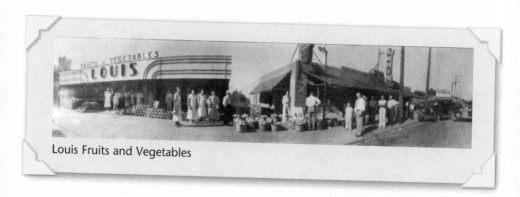

Louis Fruits and Vegetables

"Louie's." Everyone in Omaha knew Louie Paperny, and everyone called the store "Louie's Market."

Business was great, but it really took off after World War II. All four of his daughters married, and in an amazing decision that truly illuminates Louie's generosity, Zaydie gave each of his sons-in-law an equal partnership in the business.

Detail of "Admiralty in the Great State of Nebraska" certificate

Louis Market

If Bubbie was the queen of Fifty-Sixth Street, Zaydie was the king of Benson. If you had asked anyone who knew him, they would say, "Louie Paperny—a *mensch* (good guy)!" Everyone adored him—his family, his friends, his customers, his community. For a man who was short in stature, Zaydie was a huge presence, a guiding spirit in my life. This illiterate man who signed his name with an "X" was one of my greatest teachers, instructing through example, through deed, through his compassionate relationships with every human being he met.

A gregarious and ebullient man, Louie built his business on three basic principles: familiarity with your customers, huge selection, and cheap prices. When the business grew large enough in the mid-1950s, Zaydie and his four sons-in-law transformed the open-air stand into the first modern supermarket in the state of Nebraska, with self-serve aisles and checkout stands instead of counters.

I loved going up to "the market," as everyone in the family called it. Zaydie was usually at "the courtesy counter," located just inside the front door. This is where customers could cash a check, redeem pop (soda) bottles, and talk to Louie. He knew each of them by name, their family members, and their stories. And they knew him.

Zaydie grasped the importance of welcoming and public relations long before it became a science. One of his best friends in town was Father Flanagan, the priest who founded the world-famous Boys Town, located just outside Omaha; Zaydie regularly sent a truckload of food over to the kids. When he began to sell Christmas trees in the front of the store, he always sent the tallest one over to the Catholic church. When Johnny Rosenblatt, a Jewish mayor of Omaha in the 1950s, brought Triple-A baseball to town, Louie took the box right behind home plate.

Zaydie loved baseball and took me to the ballpark often to see the Omaha Cardinals, the St. Louis farm team. At the ballpark he was as big a celebrity as the players, and the players loved him. When one of them hit a home run, the stadium announcer would say, "And for hitting that homer, Lou Brock will get a twenty-five dollar gift certificate good at Louie's Market in Benson ... and folks, guess what? Louie Paperny is in the crowd tonight!"

Zaydie would rise from his seat with a huge smile on his face and wave to the crowd, while Lou Brock tipped his hat Louie's way as he crossed home plate. Pitchers, including other future stars of the St. Louis Cardinals like Bob Gibson—who worked as a sacker at Louis Market when he was in high school!—got fifty dollars in goods if they threw a shutout. We would visit the clubhouse before a game; the players would say, "You Louie's grandson? Here's a game ball; take a bat!" They treated Zaydie like royalty.

On some summer evenings I got to stay overnight at Bubbie and Zaydie's house. After dinner Zaydie would curl up on his glider on the sunporch of his house, listening to the St. Louis Cardinals game on the radio; I would watch him from the glider on the other side of the porch. Often he would fall asleep in the middle of the game, snoring loudly. Bubbie would come in to wake him up so we could go to bed. They would tuck me in and I would blissfully fall asleep, lulled by my grandparents' Yiddish lullaby:

Ai leh, lu leh,
Shluff [sleep] *mine kint* [child].
Ai leh, lu leh,
Shluff mine hartz [heart].
Ai leh, lu leh,

Shluff mine kint.
Ai leh, lu leh,
Shluff mine hartz.

The next day Zaydie would take me up to the market. I loved going to the market; growing up, it was my playground. There was an enormous, nonstop energy up and down the aisles, in the back rooms, and on the loading docks.

The coolest thing in the market was the conveyor belt system that began at the very entrance of the store next to the courtesy counter, went down into the basement, and went up again at the back door to facilitate the easy movement of heavy boxes of merchandise to the main floor for stocking the shelves. In between the belts was a labyrinth of elevated tracks of steel rollers—a roller coaster in the basement.

"C'mon, Ronnie baby!" my cousin Brucie Friedlander would yell. "Let's ride!" Brucie held an empty box while I climbed in and then hit the green button that started up the conveyor. "Hold on, Ronnie baby!" he would instruct, as he pushed me along the steel rollers and we careened around the basement. It was the closest thing to having an "E-Ticket ride" in Omaha.[*]

What really brought the crowds to Louis Market was Zaydie himself. His tagline was "Louis Sells For Less," and customers could count on rock-bottom prices in the very competitive retail environment of Omaha. Zaydie was known around town as "Carload Louie." If there was a carload of goods that needed unloading, the first call was to him. He bought carloads of watermelons, carloads of frozen fish, carloads of just about everything. Sometimes a train would derail; Louie was there to buy up the merchandise from the insurance company. Sometimes a farmer had a bumper crop; Louie would buy him out, lock, stock, and barrel. He would park a trailer full of merchandise in the parking lot of the store and sell out the back end. This emphasis on volume and selection led

---

[*] Readers of a certain age will recognize the reference to the early days of Disneyland. E-Tickets got you onto the best rides in the park.

to Louie's "five nickels" principle: he much preferred making five sales to get twenty-five cents than one sale for a quarter. So people around Omaha knew that they would get the lowest price on merchandise at Louis Market. Always.

My favorite time of year was watermelon season in the hot and humid summer of Omaha. Zaydie would get a trailer-truck-load of melons on the back lot, and he set up row upon row of ripe melons on the front plaza of the store. In front of the melons he set up wide tanks of water that looked like steel swimming pools, a couple of feet deep. In the tank Louie put huge blocks of ice and dozens of melons floating around like bobbing apples. Customers would look at the melons and judge them as if they were shopping for fish from a tank. After picking out one that looked good, Louie would take a triangular-shaped cutting device that pulled a "plug" of fruit out of the melon for the customer to taste. If she liked the melon, it was weighed on the big scale and paid for on the spot. If she didn't like it, Louie would say, "Try another one," while he sliced up the rejected melon for sale by the piece. He never let a customer leave without buying a melon—never. You got to taste them until you found one you liked.

In the spring the front plaza was a veritable nursery with hundreds of flats of flowers, and in the winter the plaza was stocked with dozens of Christmas trees. Once I was deemed old enough, I was pressed into helping out during the big rush to the holiday. I learned so much from that experience. In fact I may be the only Jewish educator in the world who can tell the difference between a Northwest pine and a Douglas fir. I can estimate the size of a tree within inches by sight (no need for a yardstick), and I can give you ten tips on how to keep your tree fresh through the New Year's holiday. It was cold, challenging work but always wonderful to help families choose a tree for their celebration.

The bar was another world. The package liquor department with its shelves of wines and spirits was in the front of the store, in the middle was the U-shaped bar, and right behind was Louis Chuck Wagon, a short-order grill offering up Louis's famous chili dogs, burgers, and fries. Because food was sold on the premises, Louis was known in Omaha as a "family bar." While sitting at the bar was forbidden to anyone under twenty-one, minors could sit in the booths that ringed the place, enjoying their chili dogs and hot tamales.

I loved sitting there looking at the ingenious advertising displays provided by the beer companies. My favorite was the Budweiser neon sign that featured a model of the Clydesdale horses pulling a wagon that circled round and round endlessly. Sometimes my mind would wander back to my earliest memories of the bar when there was sawdust on the floor, roughnecks in the seats, and a real Wild West atmosphere in the air. The décor itself was Western—mock saddle seats for the barstools, and a six-gun-toting, mustachioed cartoon character with a Stetson looking something like Yosemite Sam hawking Louis's famous twenty-five-cent beer on draft. A mural of a Western prairie scene had been painted on the back wall, complete with secret messages, like the "hidden Mickeys" at Disneyland. On the rumps of each horse was a brand: "BR," "MF," "LL," and "AW," the initials of the four uncles (Ben Rosen, Morton Friedlander, Leonard Luttbeg, Alan Wolfson) who ran Louis Market, along with Zaydie, "LP." And of course, the place reeked of smoke, though I was used to it—Dad smoked three packs of cigarettes a day.

The bar was an endlessly engaging soap opera, with a cast of characters out of some novel. There was Russ the bartender, a grizzled ex-Marine with a buzz haircut, a no-nonsense "what'll ya have" master of the bar. His wife, Lil, ran the front of the store, and the two of them were like members of the family. First stop at the bar was to say hi to Russ.

"What'll ya have, young man?" he barked.

"Coca-Cola, please," I asked.

Russ flipped open the lid of a large black refrigerated cooler, grabbed an ice-cold bottle of Coke, snapped the cap off in the opener on the front, and handed it to me.

"You in college yet?" Russ snapped, knowing full well I was only eleven.

"Not yet, Russ," I laughed. "Next year maybe."

Second stop was for Mrs. Yawel's popcorn. Mrs. Yawel was an immigrant from Russia whom Zaydie had befriended. No one is even sure how he met her. But Louie knew that the more salty popcorn his bar customers ate, the thirstier they would be. So he bought a freestanding Cretors popcorn machine, huge sacks of unpopped corn, tubs of coconut oil and salt and literally put Mrs. Yawel into business. She sat all day at the popcorn machine, making the most delicious popcorn in town. People would drive from miles around just to get some of that popcorn. She sold her brown paper bags filled with hot popcorn for ten cents a pop—so to speak—and Zaydie let her keep every penny, preferring the profit from the drinks. Mrs. Yawel put three kids through college on that popcorn machine.

Sometimes the entire family would gather for a meal at Louie's bar, commandeering a back section of the booths for a feast. Cecil, the short-order cook, would yell out the names of family members when their order was ready: "Alan, chili dogs!" One of the uncles would watch the front of the store while everyone else enjoyed the food and drink. These family gatherings usually happened quite spontaneously; one of the aunts would say, "Why don't we eat at Louie's?" to one of the other aunts on their daily phone calls to each other. And on New Year's Eve everyone would be at Louie's—as much to help out with the huge crowd as to celebrate together as a family.

It was a magical formula for business success. Five families lived off that market for many, many years. Whenever someone in the extended family needed something, there was money for it. This led to one of Bubbie's famous lines, uttered often in Yiddish: "*Louie's Market tracht aff alles*" ("Louie's Market takes care of everything"). And it did.

Of all the images I retain from my childhood experiences of Louis Market, the brightest is the full-color portrait of Zaydie on the wall above the produce department. For years, whenever I visited Omaha, I made my pilgrimage to Benson to see Zaydie's portrait. It is a particularly vivid painting, capturing his deep-blue eyes—eyes that I inherited from him and from my mother—his rough and ruddy cheeks, his stocky build, his nonexistent neck. I gaze at the portrait and overwhelming feelings of warmth embrace me, much as he would gather me into his arms in that patented leg lock of his and call me "the best boy in the United States of America." I could not have asked for a more wonderful, loving grandfather, a man of few words but many great deeds. A man who taught me life lessons through his actions—his love of family, his unabashed enjoyment of the things success brought him, his joy in giving presents, his competitiveness, his hospitality, his loyalty to employees, his patriotism. He was beloved by all who knew him, a true legend in his time.

Zaydie Louie's portrait above the bananas

Louie Paperny in front of Louis Market

Mrs. B, the Furniture Queen

Zaydie Louie was only one of the many Jewish immigrants who built amazing family businesses in Omaha. There was the Friedman family who went into the retail jewelry business, a downtown store called Borsheims. There were the other grocers—the Newmans of Hinky Dinky, the Bakers of Bakers, the Coopermans of No Frills. The wholesalers of alcohol—the Epsteins and the Friedlands. The suppliers of insecticides—the Levinson-Duitches.

But the most famous of all the merchants of Omaha was Rose Blumkin, the founder of Nebraska Furniture Mart. Mrs. B, as everyone called her, stood four foot eight, a little spark plug of a woman, who left her village in Russia when she was twenty-four years old, marrying a shoe salesman by the name of Isadore Blumkin, who fled Russia to avoid the military draft during World War I. Rose followed him to America three years later. The story goes that on her way out of Russia on the eastern border, she was stopped by a guard who would not let her pass. She told the guard, "I'm going to buy leather for the Russian army. If you let me cross, I'll bring you back the biggest bottle of vodka you ever saw." He's still waiting for the vodka.

Rose Blumkin entered the United States through Seattle with sixty-six dollars in her purse, eventually met up with Isadore in Iowa, and they moved to Omaha to begin their family. Her husband, to be kind, was not an especially successful merchant. So Rose began selling furniture out of the basement of Isadore's pawn shop in 1937. She came from the same village in Russia as Zaydie Louie—they were *landsmen*—and they had the same approach to retailing.

Mrs. B's tagline: "Sell cheap and tell the truth." Working with tiny profit margins—Mrs. B's version of Zaydie's business principle was "fast nickels are better than slow dimes"—word spread throughout the Midwest about the bargains, and the business grew rapidly.

For Mrs. B, the customer was king, queen, and president. She hated big shots, especially bankers, but she loved the lower- and middle-class folks who flocked to her new store for the ultralow prices. "I'm for the regular people." She was an instant hit. When she ran out of stock, she would sell the furniture from her own home. Once she called her daughter, a new mother, and screamed, "Empty the baby's storage chest. I got a *customer*!" Dangling from every piece of furniture in her home was a price tag, just in case.

By the 1970s, Nebraska Furniture Mart had become the largest retailer of furniture, carpeting, and appliances in the Midwest, occupying a huge seven-hundred-thousand-square-foot retail and warehouse complex on Seventy-Second Street. The place was so big that Mrs. B literally could not walk the distances on her small frame, so she took to riding through the store on an electric golf cart. By now Mrs. B, her low prices, her legendary service, and her undeniably colorful personality had personalized a fast-growing retail juggernaut.

My favorite story about Mrs. B, told by my brother Bob, illustrates an important business principle among the merchants of Omaha. In a town of that size everyone knew everyone, and many people traded with each other. For example, if Mrs. B bought groceries from her good friend Louie Paperny, she expected Louie to buy furniture from her. This principle of reciprocity was once violated by a "big shot" banker, the kind of people Mrs. B loathed.

One day Mrs. B got wind that the First National Bank of Omaha, which occupied the tallest building in town, was renovating their offices and had put out the carpeting job for bid. Mrs. B was furious. She called the bank and asked to speak to the president. As soon as he heard it was Mrs. B, the president took the call; she was, after all, one of the bank's largest account holders.

"Hallo," Mrs. B. began, in her thick Russian accent.

"Why, hello, Mrs. B," he said brightly. "How nice to speak with you."

"Are you da president of da bank?" she asked.

"Yes, Mrs. B. What can I do for you?"

"I heard about the carpeting you vant. Dat you're asking everyvone in town to give for you a bid. Is dat true?"

"Yes, Mrs. B," the president said in a voice that began to lose its enthusiastic tone.

"Tell me someting, Mr. Big Shot President"—Mrs. B's voice now began to reveal her upset—"how much money I got in your bank?"

"Well, a lot," he replied nervously.

Mrs. B shot back, "You gotta *truck*? If you don't gotta truck, I got plenty. I'll send von over right now to get mine money."

Suffice it to say, the call for bids to carpet the bank was withdrawn and Mrs. B got the business. By any measure Nebraska Furniture Mart was a huge success and caught the eye of an investor in Omaha—Warren E. Buffett, the famous "Oracle of Omaha," one of the richest men in the world. After Buffett had closed his investment group and took control of a holding company, Berkshire Hathaway, he looked for businesses to buy. Once he walked into Nebraska Furniture Mart and made an offer to buy the store. Mrs. B turned him down flat with a two-word answer: "Too cheap." On his fifty-third birthday, August 30, 1983, Buffett tracked her down in the carpeting department, Mrs. B's favorite domain. He was determined to buy the store as a birthday present to himself and his shareholder "owners."

"Mrs. B," Buffett began, "I want to buy the store."

"How much you gonna pay?" Mrs. B asked.

Buffett had already run some numbers by Louie Blumkin, Mrs. B's son.

"Sixty million dollars," Buffett said.

Mrs. B stuck out her stubby little hand.

"Okay, Mr. Buffett, vee gotta deal."

Buffett rushed back to his office and drafted a two-page agreement, buying 90 percent of the company, leaving the Blumkin family with 10 percent—a common practice for him to keep the original managers in place and motivated. The next day he brought Mrs. B a check. There was no audit of the books, no taking inventory, no lawyers. Just a simple handshake—the way many of the merchants of Omaha did deals.

By all accounts, Mrs. B was driven, stubborn, and occasionally difficult. While she loved her employees and they were unusually loyal to her—many of them spent their entire working lives at NFM—she would regularly call them names and berate them for not selling cheap enough. She would get upset and fire employees; Louie B would hire them back. In 1989, when the carpeting department had lost money for three years running, Mrs. B was stripped of her authority. She went ballistic and quit. She sat at home for several months and then decided to start all over again—right across the street! She owned a building directly opposite Nebraska Furniture Mart and, in no time, called her suppliers and opened as "Mrs. B's Warehouse." She was ninety-five years old. All of Omaha was flabbergasted by the very public family spat. Mrs. B's Warehouse did well, but in 1992 the family resolved the dispute. Mrs. B sold the building to Buffett for *another* $5 million cash, and there was once again peace on Seventy-Second Street. Buffett wrote to his stockholders, "This time around, Mrs. B graciously offered to sign a non-compete agreement—and I, having been incautious on this point when she was 89, snapped at the deal. Mrs. B belongs in the *Guinness Book of World Records* on many counts. Signing a non-compete at 99 merely adds one more."

Warren Buffett and Rose Blumkin

My Hour with Warren Buffett

Whenever people hear I am from Omaha, the first thing they want to know is if I have met Warren Buffett. The answer is yes. I spent an hour with Mr. Buffet in August 2006, the kind of private meeting for which a man from Singapore paid $2.3 million in 2014 as the winner of a charity auction benefitting the Glide Foundation. I had the opportunity to meet with him because of my rabbi.

Myer S. Kripke, the rabbi of my youth, was a short, humble man and an intellectual—quiet, formal, reserved—unless he was playing shortstop at the annual Beth El Synagogue family picnic. His children were a precocious bunch: Saul became the most important philosopher of the late twentieth century, a man so advanced in his field no one could give him a PhD, since his thinking and writing were far superior to those of any of his professors. Madeline became an expert in dictionaries, collecting some twenty thousand of them in her New York City apartment and nearby warehouses. Netta became a successful psychotherapist. But it was Rabbi Kripke's wife, Dorothy, who connected the Kripkes and the Buffetts.

Dorothy Karp and Myer Kripke had met as students at the Jewish Theological Seminary in New York City, where after a courtship they were married in the courtyard. Rabbi Kripke accepted pulpits in Connecticut, then Ohio, and eventually settled in Omaha to serve the Conservative synagogue, Beth El. There the Kripkes lived in a synagogue-owned three-story brick home on Happy Hollow Boulevard, just a few houses from Dodge Street, the main thoroughfare in the city.

In 1953 Dorothy wrote a children's book titled *Let's Talk About God*. My mother, who adored and admired her *rebbetzin* (rabbi's spouse), read the book aloud to me often; it was one of my very favorites. To this day it is the best book ever written to explain to children the concept of a God that cannot be seen, but whose impact in the world is quite visible:

> We cannot see God.... We cannot see many things. We cannot see the wind. But we see autumn leaves flying and dancing, all orange and gold. We see a bright green kite sailing in the sky. Then we know the wind is there. We see what the wind does, even though we cannot see the wind itself. We cannot see love, but we know when someone loves us. We feel love in a hug or a smile or a friendly look or a warm touch. We feel love in many ways, but we never see love. We cannot see God. But we do see what God does in the world.... We cannot see God, but we know that God is there.

One day Susie Buffett, Warren's wife, walked into the home of one of the Kripkes' congregants who sold books and educational toys out of her basement, looking for a gift for her daughter, also named Susie. There in the corner sat a stack of *Let's Talk About God*. Susie Buffett bought a copy and read the book to her daughter, who, like me, loved it. When she learned that the author was from Omaha, Mrs. Buffett invited Mrs. Kripke for coffee.

Little did Dorothy know, it was a coffee destined to change her life. The two women shared their stories and discovered mutual interests. They both enjoyed literature. They both were raising a family. They both loved to play bridge. And as it turns out, they were neighbors; their homes were within a block of each other. At the end of the coffee date, the two women resolved to meet again, this time with their husbands.

The Kripkes and the Buffetts became fast friends, their close relationship growing over the years. The foursome played regular games of bridge, Netta was a regular babysitter for "Little Susie" as she was called, and the Buffetts invited the Kripkes to share

Thanksgiving dinner every year. When Susie Buffett learned that the rabbi's family would have to pass on the nonkosher turkey, she hired a gourmet chef to make tuna salad for them. When Dorothy became disabled, it was Susie who drove her to physical therapy. Warren and the rabbi were both members of Rotary and shared a passion for ideas.

By the mid-1960s Warren had made his mark in Omaha with his successful investment groups. The bar for admission was high: minimum $100,000 cash and no say in how the money was to be invested. The Kripkes had inherited some money from an uncle and saved a bit of their own. Dorothy encouraged the rabbi to ask Warren to invest their modest nest egg of some $67,000. He resisted: "It's not enough, and I don't want to mix business with friendship." Susie told Warren, "You've got a minister and a priest in your group. It couldn't hurt to have a rabbi!" It took three years before the rabbi finally asked, but when he did, Warren readily agreed. "I liked Myer," Buffett said. "I wanted people who, if it went bad, we could still be friends."

It didn't go bad. Buffett's investors reaped an enormous return on their money—an annual compounded rate of 31 percent. When Warren decided to close the group in 1970, some of his investors received shares in Berkshire Hathaway. The stock was worth about forty dollars per share. The rabbi told me, "When the share price went from forty to fifty dollars, I sold some shares, thinking I would never see that kind of profit again. Then the shares went to sixty dollars and I bought them back."

Typical of the rabbi and Dorothy, they told nobody in Omaha about their investment. No one at the synagogue knew that their rabbi was becoming fabulously wealthy. Nothing changed about the rabbi's lifestyle. "Dorothy once asked me, 'Would you like to buy a better car?'" he recalled. "I said, 'There's nothing wrong with a Chevrolet.'" Even when the rabbi was unceremoniously urged into early retirement after serving the congregation for thirty-six years, no one knew—that is, until the Kripkes called their alma mater, the Jewish Theological Seminary, and asked a development officer to come to Omaha to discuss a gift. Seven million dollars later, the Kripkes agreed to help rebuild the seminary's library tower, which had been destroyed in a terrible fire in 1966, the same year the Kripkes invested with Buffett.*

Well before anyone knew of their wealth, my mother had a long and wonderful relationship with the Kripkes. She was a good friend to Dorothy, especially when Dorothy fell ill with a neurological disorder that rendered her nearly blind and bedridden most of the time. Mom would bring over homemade cabbage soup, kugels, and other Jewish delicacies. She was furious with Beth El Synagogue when some young folks forced the rabbi into retirement.

When Dorothy Kripke died in 2000 and the rabbi moved into a suite of rooms at the Rose Blumkin Jewish Home in Omaha, Mom called the rabbi every night, just to check in, to see if he needed anything. She invited the rabbi to family Passover Seders, Rosh Hashanah meals, and Yom Kippur break-fasts. She bought him suits and shirts and made sure he was receiving world-class care. When Mom died, my father made daily visits to the rabbi, bringing him his favorite chocolates and ice cream, schmoozing with him for hours, sharing stories in Yiddish and listening to the rabbi's jokes.

"Do you know this one, Alan? A British Jew is waiting in line to be knighted by the queen. He is to kneel in front of her and recite a sentence in Latin when she taps him on the shoulder with her sword. When his turn comes, he panics in the excitement of the moment and forgets the Latin. Thinking quickly, he recites the only other sentence he knows in a foreign language—from the Passover Seder: '*Mah nishtanah ha-lailah ha-zeh mi-kol ha-leilot.*'

"Puzzled, the queen turns to her advisor and asks, 'Why is this knight different from all other knights?'"**

---

* At the time of this—the largest donation in the history of the seminary—Berkshire Hathaway shares were worth $55,000 each. Today, they trade at more than $220,000 *per share.*

** The literal translation of *Mah nishtanah ha-lailah ha-zeh mi-kol ha-leilot* is "How different is this *night* from all other nights!"

On my visits to Omaha, I too would visit with Rabbi Kripke at the Blumkin Home, regaling him with stories of my travels and my teaching, sharing copies of my books, soliciting his feedback, and hoping for his approval. Frankly he was somewhat amazed that the *vildeh chayeh* who spent many hours sitting in his study after being thrown out of class had become a Jewish educator of some repute. He was always kind, always proud, and I looked forward to our visits and weekly phone calls every Friday afternoon to wish him, "*Guht Shabbes.*"

In 2004 Mom organized a gala ninetieth birthday party for Rabbi Kripke, and I was tapped to be the master of ceremonies. Warren Buffett was on the guest list, and he arrived along with his daughter, Susie. This was my first opportunity to meet the great Oracle of Omaha. Charming and witty, he offered a heartfelt and funny toast to his friend, telling the crowd of family and friends how proud he was of the rabbi's philanthropic efforts.

Two years later I came to the rabbi with an idea to honor Dorothy's groundbreaking work in Jewish children's literature. "Let's establish a National Jewish Book Award in her memory," I suggested. "One of the best ways Jewish parents can share Jewish information and values with children is by reading aloud a good Jewish children's book. Like Dorothy did in *Let's Talk About God*, the author gives parents the words they often struggle to find on their own, and the act of reading together strengthens the family bonds."

"I love the idea, Ron," Rabbi said. "Let's do it."

We created the Dorothy K. and Myer S. Kripke Institute for Jewish Family Literacy as a nonprofit entity to supervise the effort. I flew to Omaha, checked the rabbi out of the Blumkin Home, and accompanied him to New York City to witness the Jewish Book Council annual dinner and ceremony at which the first National Jewish Book Award in Jewish family literature in memory of Dorothy Kripke was bestowed.

In August of that same year I was visiting family in Omaha and made my usual appointment to see Rabbi Kripke. As we were chatting, an idea came to me. Perhaps his friend Warren would be interested in supporting the Kripke Institute? Rabbi thought it was a great idea and offered to call to set up an appointment. Warren answered his own phone: "Of course, Myer. I would be happy to meet with you and your protégé."

When we arrived at the headquarters of Berkshire Hathaway, Warren immediately escorted us into his modest office. He was warm and welcoming, thrilled to see his friend Myer again. After chatting with him for a few minutes, he turned to me. "Tell me your story, Ron." I shared my connection to Louie Paperny and the grocery business, and we chatted about his uncle's grocery store in Dundee, not five blocks from where I grew up. I noticed a photo of him throwing out the first pitch at a St. Louis Cardinals game in Busch Stadium, so we talked baseball for a while. Once again I found the man charming, witty, and completely engaging, a down-to-earth Midwesterner who wore his wealth like a comfortable sweater.

"Warren," I said, "I must tell you that wherever I travel in the world, when people hear I'm from Omaha, Nebraska, the first thing they want to know is if I know you. I tell them about our first meeting at Rabbi Kripke's ninetieth birthday celebration and then share stories about you. My favorite is the one told to me about the Berkshire annual meeting a few years ago. After the introductory film, you and Charlie Munger answered questions from the stockholders for six hours. That day a woman reached a microphone and said, 'Mr. Buffett, I'm almost embarrassed to ask you a question; I only own one share of Berkshire Hathaway.' You didn't miss a beat. You answered, 'Madam, never underestimate the value of your holdings. Between you and me, we control this company!'"

Buffett laughed. "Yes, I remember that exchange."

As the hour drew to a close, Rabbi Kripke told Warren about the new Kripke Institute and asked if he would be interested in participating. Buffett was prepared with what was surely his standard answer to requests for funding: "Myer, Ron, you know, I learned a long time ago to only do the things I know how to do. I know how to make dough; I don't know how to give it away. That's why I gave most of my money to Bill Gates. He's spending the rest of his life building a foundation that will give the money to worthy causes. If I could, I would give it all for nuclear disarmament and population control; these are the two things that most threaten our planet. So, I'm sorry I cannot participate in your worthy endeavor. Why don't you raise it with my daughter, Susie? She's interested in education."

While disappointed, I did not want the hour to end on a downer. So I said, "Well, Warren, we understand. But before we leave, I need to tell you how thrilled everyone in the Jewish community is with your recent purchase of ISCAR, the tool-making company in Israel, for four billion dollars. I understand the sale will result in one billion dollars in tax revenue to the Israeli government. And I hear that you are planning to go to Israel soon! Is that really happening?"

"Yes, it is, Ron," Buffett replied. "I'm going in September, in just a few weeks. Susie is not all that thrilled that I'm going now, but I promised, so I will."*

"Well, Warren," I replied, "it's wonderful that you are going. It's quite a place. You know, the first time I told someone I was going to Israel, the person took out his wallet and gave me money to take."

"What's that all about, Ron?" Warren asked.

"Oh, it's an old Jewish tradition. If you meet someone going to Israel, you give the person money to give to someone in need over there. Whoever gets the money thinks it's coming from the pilgrim to Israel, but it's not. It's coming from the original donor, which makes it an anonymous gift. In the Jewish tradition, this is the highest level of what we call *tzedakah*, righteous giving. And, in addition, God will protect you on your journey."

And then I took out my wallet and I, Ron Wolfson, gave Warren Buffett a dollar bill. And he took it!

"Well, Ron, I'll be happy to give this to someone there. Thank you," Warren said.

I was thrilled. As we were leaving his office, I was too embarrassed to ask Warren for an autograph in front of Rabbi Kripke. So

---

* That summer, the Israelis fought a brief war with Hezbollah, a terrorist group that had captured three Israeli soldiers, and tensions were still high in the region.

instead I wrote him a handwritten letter when I returned to Los Angeles, thanking him for the visit and asking him for an autograph "for my grandchildren." Within a few weeks I received a letter in response, telling me about his trip to Israel (he was a huge hit). Enclosed was a small business card featuring a cartoon caricature of Buffett, complete with horn-rimmed glasses and bushy eyebrows. The inscription reads:

> To Ron, who has the same Rabbi as I do.
> Warren E. Buffett

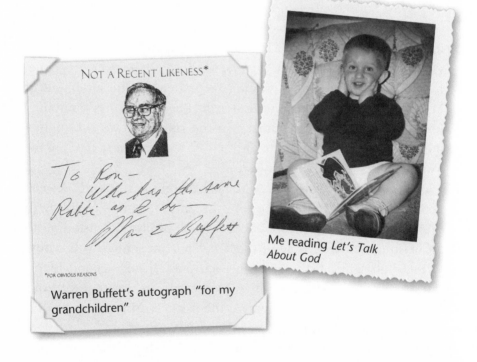

Warren Buffett's autograph "for my grandchildren"

Me reading *Let's Talk About God*

S. K.

Omaha was a wonderful place to grow up, even if some may think it provincial. Of the many treasures I discovered there, the one I cherish most is a European import.

One Sunday afternoon during a youth group meeting, the youth director—Mar Molad as we called him (*mar* means "mister" in Hebrew)—announced a joint event between USY and the youth group from Beth Israel, the nearby Modern Orthodox synagogue. It was a Bible Quiz Bowl evening to be held in the basement of Marsha Elkon's house in the center of "Bagel," the predominantly Jewish neighborhood of Omaha in the sixties. It was the night I met the love of my life. Little did I know, she was there to meet *me*. I was just lucky enough to show up.

Susie Kukawka was one of Marsha Elkon's best friends. A week before the Bible Quiz Bowl event, she and Marsha were sitting in the Lewis and Clark Junior High School auditorium listening to a Christmas concert. One of the songs was presented by the Boys Octet, eight guys, two voices on each part. I sang second tenor. We wore Perry Como–style baby-blue cardigan sweaters with our names appliquéd in felt letters on the pockets. Mine read: RON. I seem to remember the song was "Winter Wonderland."

For some reason, Susie noticed me. "Who is that guy?" she asked Marsha.

"Oh, that's Ron Wolfson. He's in my youth group at the synagogue."

"He really loves what he's doing," Susie observed.

"You wanna meet him?" Marsha asked.

"How?"

"My youth group is having a program Saturday night at my house. It's perfect. He'll be there. A lot of other nice guys, too."

"Okay. Sure. I'll come," Susie decided.

When I walked down the stairs to Marsha's basement that Saturday night, I noticed Susie immediately. "What a cute girl!" I thought to myself. "I wonder who she is?"

I wasted no time approaching her. A smidgeon over five feet tall, with beautiful brown eyes and a smile that lit up the room, she was wearing an Indian madras blouse; madras was all the rage in 1963—the fabric actually "bled" in the wash, creating an endless variety of plaid patterns. I was fashionably wearing a button-down Gant shirt, with the little loop on the back, and Canoe cologne. Her initials—"S. K."—had been embroidered on the breast pocket of her shirt. I couldn't help but notice—the initials, that is.

"Hi, I'm Ron," I blurted out.

"Hi, I'm Susie," she smiled.

"Susie who?" I asked.

"Susie Kukawka," she replied. "It means 'cuckoo bird.' In Polish." I thought that was the coolest name ever, especially when she spelled it for me. "The 'w' is pronounced as an 'f,'" Susie explained. "Like 'Kafka' with a 'koo' in front of it. Koo-Kafka, that's how you say it."

Cute girl. Cute name. It was love at first sight. I was fifteen. She was fourteen.

I did not leave her side the rest of the evening. I was totally smitten.

I invited her to come to the synagogue the next Friday night. It wasn't exactly a date, but at that age most of us were just hanging out together. My strategy was to get her involved in my youth group and go from there. At this I was extraordinarily successful.

Susie and I soon became an item. Within a couple of weeks I met her parents, Hilde and Abe, two Holocaust survivors who had met in Berlin after World War II. They married in 1948 and in 1950 gave birth to their little "Sure" (pronounced "sue-reh"), Susie's given Yiddish name. In 1951 the three of them, along with Abe's brother Gedalia (George), immigrated to the United States, entering though the port of New Orleans, assigned to live in Fort Worth, Texas, by the Jewish immigration agency, HIAS. Unlike many immigrants, they had no sponsors, no relatives. When they arrived in New Orleans, the HIAS representative in charge of placing immigrants told them the quota for Fort Worth had been filled and offered them a spot in Omaha, Nebraska, instead. "You'll like it; the weather there is more like Poland than Texas," the agent assured them. They had no idea where any city was, so readily agreed. To this day Susie says the real reason they ended up in Omaha was so she could meet me.

We had a whirlwind romance, and I began to spend a lot of time at Susie's house on Sixty-First Street. Abe Kukawka worked long hours at the Sperry factory making hydraulic pumps, while Hilde was a homemaker. They both spoke with thick accents, so their only child, Susie, was the family mouthpiece. She was recruited to answer the phones, make calls to vendors, and speak for her parents. German and Yiddish were spoken in the house. Although they belonged to the Modern Orthodox synagogue, most of their observance in the home was relegated to holidays and keeping kosher. Abe went to services only on the High Holy Days, mainly to say *Kaddish* for his parents, three sisters, and their families in Slawatycze, who were all murdered by the Nazis. Hilde had been hidden by a compassionate Christian family, just outside of Berlin, during the entire period of the war. Amazingly Susie knew virtually nothing of this history—a common experience of survivors' children—until I showed up and began asking questions. For hours Abe and Hilde would amaze me with their stories; Susie sat slack-jawed in awe as her family secrets were revealed.

"How did you meet?" I asked one day.

"I went to a Jewish community center one Friday night with my best friend, Ruth, also a Berliner," Hilde recalled. "In walk two guys from Poland—Abe and his best friend, Lova Bornstein.

Before you know it, Abe and I were a couple and so were Ruth and Lova. We both were married and began our families."

"Oh, we had a wonderful time then," Abe said. "You could buy a Leica camera with a few cartons of cigarettes. Lova and I were working the black market, making lots of money ..."

"... and getting drunk," Hilde revealed. "Lova would see someone he thought was a Nazi who killed his parents, and he would run them over with his car. Abe had to bail him out of jail all the time. Ruth had a baby, Avremeleh, and I had a baby, Sureleh, and we decided we better get out of that city. So we got visas to America, and the Bornsteins got visas to Australia."

"When we arrived at immigration in New Orleans," Abe said, "the officer told me, 'You can't be 'Kukawka' in America. Nobody can pronounce it.' He wanted me to change my name. I told him, 'They took away my home. They took my parents and my sisters and their children and murdered them. You're not taking away my name!'"

Susie and I had been dating for more than a year when, during a summer family vacation in Wisconsin, I flirted with another girl. It was a meaningless fling; I can't even remember the girl's name. I was so embarrassed when I returned to Omaha, I couldn't face Susie. I didn't call her to break up; I didn't want to break up, but I felt intensely guilty. Instead I did something even more stupid: I ignored her. Whenever I saw her in the halls of Central High, I turned the other way.

Susie could not understand what was happening. She hadn't done anything or said anything to turn me away. She thought we had something good going. Why the sudden cold shoulder? She could have—and probably should have—written me off, moved on. There were plenty of guys—some of my best friends, actually—who would have gladly taken my place alongside this cute, wonderful girl. But that's not Susie.

One afternoon as I was walking between classes, I suddenly felt a tug at the collar of my shirt. Someone was putting a note down my back. As I turned around to see who it was, I glimpsed Susie, moving swiftly in the opposite direction. I pulled out my shirttails, and the note tumbled to the floor. I picked it up and read it on the spot. It was a handwritten poem, titled "Look Away":

> Why is it when I see you,
> You always look away?
> Why is it that I find myself
> Without a word to say?
> I know exactly what to say
> Before I see you come;
> It's just right after seeing you
> That makes me feel so dumb!
> Without a wave or "Hi" or smile
> You pass me by so fast—
> And when I ask you why this is
> You say, "I think of my next class."
> Although whene'er I see you,
> Our eyes may go astray;
> I'll still be searching for the day
> When we won't look away.

My body shook with goose bumps as I read the amazing poem. I took it as a plea for me to reengage her, to explain myself. Maybe— I hoped—this was an opportunity for me to ask for forgiveness, maybe even to rekindle our relationship. I really did love her, and it didn't feel like puppy love.

I went home that day, retreated to my bedroom, and read the poem over and over again, trying to decipher what Susie was telling me. I kept focusing on the last lines, "I'll still be searching for the day when we won't look away." It took me two days to gather the courage to call her, to ask her out for a talk, to reignite our romance. She was angry, of course. Not as angry as her father, who was furious at the way I had treated his daughter. I begged her to start anew, I sent her flowers and stuffed animals and letters expressing my affection. I asked her out on a date and tried to make amends. In those moments my love for "my Susaleh" grew and grew. Within a few weeks she had forgiven me.

I never looked away again.

Hilde, Abe, and their Suraleh in Berlin, just before immigrating to the United States of America

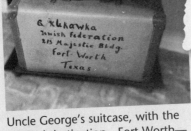

Uncle George's suitcase, with the original destination—Fort Worth—written on the side

Young love

Der Rosenkavalier

By the time I left Omaha for college at Washington University in St. Louis, I knew Susie was my *basherte*, my intended one. She was one year behind me in school, and I didn't want her to have a miserable time during her senior year, so I encouraged her to date, but not too seriously. I traveled from St. Louis to Omaha as many weekends as possible to spend with her. When Susie enrolled as a freshman at the University of Nebraska–Lincoln the following year, once again I took the position that she could date, but I called her every Saturday night just after the eleven o'clock curfew to see if she had returned to her dorm. I sent her flowers on our "anniversary" of going out together, the twenty-sixth of each month. Roses. Susie's mom called me *der Rosenkavalier* (the knight of the rose).

By 1969 I hatched a plan for us to be together in St. Louis, talking her parents into letting her transfer to the University of Missouri–St. Louis. This was to be the ultimate test of our relationship: could we live together? Well, not "live-in" live together; I was the in-house caretaker of the Washington University Hillel House living in an apartment on the third floor of the building, and Susie was boarding nearby. But within three weeks of us being together in St. Louis, I knew it was time to ask her the big question.

I called my parents to tell them of my decision to ask Susie to marry me. They, of course, were overjoyed, and my mother set about finding an appropriate diamond engagement ring. I told Susie I needed to go to Omaha by myself to take an insurance physical; she bought the ruse completely. The real purpose of the trip was to ask her parents' blessing for our union. They were thrilled as well. "But keep it a secret," I warned. I had planned a creative way to pop the question, and I didn't want anyone spilling the beans to Susie.

So on a cloudy Wednesday in November, Susie Kukawka and Ron Wolfson were booked on a one-hour flight from St. Louis to Omaha on Braniff Airlines. As we boarded, I had placed my hanging bag in a closet near the front of the plane. We made our way to a window and middle seat near the rear of the McDonnell-Douglas Super 80 jet, an eight-year-old boy sitting next to us on the aisle. Susie was a bundle of nerves; it was her first visit home since her transfer from Lincoln to St. Louis. I was also nervous, but for another reason, a reason Susie had no inkling of. As we began the initial descent, I told Susie I needed to retrieve something from my hanging bag. When I reached the closet, the flight attendant tried to shoo me back to my seat, but I whispered something in her ear; she smiled and helped me reach the bag. I grabbed my hidden package and returned with it, sat down, and handed it to Susie.

"What's this?" she asked.

"A present ... for you," I answered proudly.

"Ronnie, we're landing! I can't open a present now!"

"Susie, open the present," I insisted, while the little boy next to us began to pay attention to what was unfolding.

The present was a beautifully wrapped floral package. As Susie opened it, she discovered a single long-stemmed red rose.

"Happy anniversary," I chirped, reminding her that the twenty-sixth of the month was our monthly "anniversary," which, without fail, I marked by giving Susie a single red rose.

"Oh, Ronnie," she said, somewhat perturbed, "but I can't concentrate on this now! We're about to meet our parents!"

"I know, honey," I said calmly. "Smell the rose."

Reluctantly Susie held the bud to her nose and quickly turned her face to the window to see how soon we would land.

"Susie," I insisted, "*look* at the rose."

She really was not at all interested in examining the rose, a present she received monthly. But she did.

"Very nice, Ronnie. Thank you."

"Honey, look *inside* the rose!" I pleaded.

When she finally did, she let out a gasp, for inside the bud of the rose was a two-carat marquis-cut diamond ring, the kind we had been looking at in jewelry stores. I had taken the ring to a florist, explained the idea, and she brilliantly attached the ring to the stem of the rose with a pipe cleaner.

"Read the card," I instructed Susie.

She opened the envelope attached to the rose. In Hebrew, I had written the words *V'eirastikh li l'olam*—"Be betrothed to me forever" (from Hosea 2:21). I suppose it was an indication of how far I had come in my Jewish awareness. I am unsure whether Susie knew the meaning of the words, but the look on her face once she realized what was happening said, *I want the traditional "ask," Ronnie!*

In the impossibly cramped space of an airplane seat, there was no way to get down on one knee, so I grasped her hands, looked into her deep-brown eyes, and said, "Susie Kukawka, will you marry me?"

Susie whispered, "Yes!" and we kissed while the boy sitting next to us looked on, bewildered.

Just then, the wheels touched down at Eppley Airfield. The flight attendant came on the PA system and said, "Ladies and gentleman, Braniff International Airlines welcomes you to Omaha, Nebraska. Please keep your seat belts fastened until we reach the gate. We hope you enjoyed our short flight from St. Louis. We know a couple in the back of the plane—Ron and Susie—did. They just became engaged to be married!"

The entire plane erupted in applause. The little boy suddenly understood what had transpired. People looked around to catch a glimpse of us, the happy couple. By then I had untied the ring from the pipe cleaner stem and placed it on Susie's ring finger, where it shown brilliantly in the setting-sun rays streaming through the window of the fuselage. The plane had made its descent, but our hearts were still soaring.

When we reached the gate, everyone began to exit the plane through the stairs in the rear of the MD-80 aircraft. These were the days before Omaha had jet bridges. In fact it was still a time when those welcoming visitors could actually stand on the tarmac to greet passengers. Sitting near the rear, by rights we should have been among the first people off. But my hanging bag was still in the closet in the front of the plane, so we had to wait in place. As people walked by, they smiled and congratulated us; it was our first receiving line!

Meanwhile we were not getting off the plane, and our entire family—parents, brothers, aunts, uncles, cousins, and of course Zaydie and Bubbie—were standing on the tarmac waiting for us, wondering, "Where are Ronnie and Susie? Maybe she said no?" Finally the last of the passengers walked past our row, I retrieved the hanging bag, and we walked down the stairs, rushing into the waiting arms of our joyous family. Once everyone hugged and kissed, we were whisked away to a hotel for a huge engagement party, where the celebration continued well into the night. I've always loved a good surprise—and this was a doozy!

✡

Our engagement portrait.
Isn't she cute?!

On June 21, 1970, Susie and I were married at Beth Israel Synagogue in Omaha in front of three hundred family and friends. It was a beautiful wedding, marred only by the uninvited appearance of a guy who was infatuated with Susie. She handled him sensitively, meeting with him in the hallway of the synagogue. It's one of the many things I love about Susie: she cares for others far more than she cares about herself.

In those days newlyweds could not wait to leave the wedding and start the honeymoon. It was certainly true of us. I mean, the wedding night was a big deal. Today the bride and groom sweep the floors—they are the last to leave the reception. What's the urgency when you've been living together for eight years? Not for Susie and me. We left the synagogue at 10:00 p.m. in our "going-away" outfits, now terribly dated. Ours were summer pastels to match our brand-new luggage—a bright-turquoise flowery paisley print.

After the big send-off from the family and wedding guests, we headed for the Holiday Inn of Omaha, where we had booked the honeymoon suite. But some astronaut was visiting the city, so we were bumped to the Casbah Suite—don't ask! The only thing I remember is some sort of tentlike canopy over the bed.

Everything was going fine until I picked up the brand-new suitcase—and the handle broke off! This was a problem because the next morning we were going to meet the family for breakfast and a bon voyage as we boarded a plane for our honeymoon destination, Disneyland. But I couldn't pick up this huge suitcase, and I didn't know what to do. There was no way we could go on the trip like that. So now it was about 11:30 p.m.—on our wedding night—and I decided there was only one thing to do: I called my father.

Handyman, gardener, inventor, philosopher, Dad was my go-to guy in times of trouble. Although Mom ruled the roost, much like her mother dominated my grandparents' home, Dad always seemed to know how to fix things, a problem solver. And, boy, did I have a problem.

Dad answered the phone in a voice that wondered, *who could be calling at this hour?*

"Hello?"

"Dad?"

"*Ronnie?*" He couldn't believe it was me on the phone—calling from our wedding bed.

"What's the matter! Is everything okay?"

I blurted out the first thing that came to mind: "Dad, I need a screwdriver ..."

After a beat, we both dissolved into laughter. As soon as I explained what happened, he assured me that the suitcase problem would be solved. He brought a whole tool chest to the airport, fixed the handle, and we had a great time on the honeymoon.

Dancing at the wedding with Zaydie Louie

A Rabbi, Maybe?

After our honeymoon, we moved into an apartment in Olivette, a suburb of St. Louis. Susie prepared for her courses in early childhood and elementary education at the University of Missouri–St. Louis, and I began thinking more seriously about my professional aspirations.

In high school, when I'd traveled to different synagogues in the Midwest as president of USY, I quickly ascertained that the position of rabbi occupied the top rung of the congregational staff. In fact, although I had been groomed to be a businessman or entrepreneur, I began to envision myself becoming a rabbi. No way would I be a Jewish educator like Mr. Friedman.

When I began to share this idea with my closest family and advisors, the response was warm. Mom loved the idea. Dad too.

Zaydie Louie, however, had his doubts: "Too many bosses." When I persisted that I thought the rabbinate was my calling, he said, "First, make a million dollars. Then, become a rabbi."

But I was hooked. I spent two of my college summers at the Jewish Theological Seminary in New York City, studying for my entrance exams for rabbinical school, including the momentous summer of 1969—a hot, intense time, punctuated by the moon landing, Woodstock, the Manson murders, and a weeklong visit from Susie; I wanted to convince her that we would be happy living in New York as I studied to become a rabbi. I saved up money, bought tickets to eight Broadway shows, took her to the "21" Club for dinner (I could only afford two appetizers—something that

came in gefilte fish jelly), and made the big mistake of taking a sub-
way at rush hour. She was unimpressed, but I soldiered on.

To be admitted to the seminary, I was required to take exams
in Talmud, Bible, and Hebrew and be interviewed by a panel of
rabbis to assess my character as a future preacher and teacher. I
managed to pass the tests by the end of the summer and was then
invited to sit for the nerve-racking interview. How ironic! "*Sheket*"
Wolfson interviewing for rabbinical school.

This was a big deal. There were plenty of guys who had passed
the exams but failed to impress the rabbinic panel. This forty-five-
minute interview would determine my life's path. On a Friday
morning, dressed in a suit and tie, I was led by my advisor, Rabbi
Joe Brodie, into a large conference room in the Teacher's Institute
building. There, around a huge square table, sat twenty-five rabbis
wearing *kippot* (head coverings), most with beards, looking rather
somber and serious. There were no name tags, no name tents; the
only two people in the room I knew by name were Rabbi Brodie and
the dean of the rabbinical school, Rabbi Neil Gillman. I was directed
to the hot seat next to Rabbi Brodie. Seated directly across from me
was a regal-looking gentleman, tall, with snowy white hair and horn-
rimmed glasses. He did not introduce himself to me, but it was clear
he was the chairman of the panel and quickly began the interview.

"Welcome, Mr. Wolfson," he said, looking through my file
with its academic transcripts and letters of recommendation. "I
see you are studying at Washington University in St. Louis. Tell us,
please, what courses are you enrolled in?"

"Well," I replied nervously, "I am studying Jewish history and
philosophy with Steven Schwarzschild."

"Oh, Schwarzschild," the chairman interrupted. "Good man."
Several of the rabbis around the table nodded in agreement. I took
this as a good sign. "And I see you are studying Hebrew. How is
that going?"

"It's fine," I said. "We're studying Biblical Hebrew."

"Biblical Hebrew, eh?" the chairman asked, his curiosity
piqued. "What book are you using?"

"Well, it's a thin little book with a blue cover," I replied. "It's problematic."

"Problematic, you say?" the chairman leaned in. "How so?"

"Well," I stammered, "the problem is not the Hebrew. It's the English." As I was offering this critique, my eyes caught sight of the rabbis around the table. While they seemed pleasant enough at the beginning of the interrogation, now their heads began to slump, their eyes looking down at the table. I sensed something was going awry, but I had no clue why.

The chairman now had his hook in me. "What is the problem with the English?" he asked.

"Well, the author is a grammarian, and the technical language he uses is, well, it's *incomprehensible*." Suddenly, the tension in the room was palpable. I looked over to Rabbi Brodie, but his gaze avoided mine. Several of the rabbis seemed to be sweating.

"Incomprehensible, eh?" the chairman shouted. "Tell us, Mr. Wolfson, what is the name of this incomprehensible book?"

"*Introduction to Biblical Hebrew*," I reported confidently. Several of the rabbis began coughing. Rabbi Brodie looked at me plaintively, as if to say, "You've really got yourself in a hole."

The chairman was not done. "And, Mr. Wolfson," my anonymous inquisitor growled, "who is the *author* of this incomprehensible book?"

"Let me think," I stammered, trying to remember the author's name, thinking to myself, *Who remembers the names of college textbook authors?*

"Green ... stein? Green ... sweig? I know it's Green ... something ..." I looked around the table. One rabbi's face was beet red. Several rabbis were completely slumped in their chairs. Even Rabbi Brodie was *shvitzing* (sweating). I thought to myself, *They are embarrassed that I don't know the author's name. I better get it right.* So in that split second I tried to envision the thin little blue book in my mind's eye, looking below the title for the elusive name.

"Greenberg!" I shouted. "It's Greenberg! That's it—Greenberg!"

There was total silence. No one was looking at me; every rabbi was looking to the chairman, waiting for his reaction. With the expert timing of a practiced performer, he hesitated for just a moment, then slammed his hand on the table in front of him, and let out ... an uproarious laugh!

"Ha, ha, ha!" he bellowed. "I told my son Moshe the same thing when he wrote that book! Incomprehensible, indeed!"

Suddenly all the anonymous rabbis in the room began laughing, taking their cue from their leader, the famous vice chancellor of the Jewish Theological Seminary, the dean of the Conservative rabbis, the much-admired, greatly respected Rabbi Simon Greenberg. His son, Moshe Greenberg, the eminent Bible scholar and professor at Hebrew University in Jerusalem, was in fact the author of *Introduction to Biblical Hebrew*. I learned all this from a relieved Rabbi Brodie, who whispered the information to me as the room rocked with laughter.

Rabbi Greenberg, tickled by this trap he had laid for me, turned to his colleagues: "I told Moshe, 'You've written a wonderful guide to biblical grammar, but your use of the technical language will be an obstacle for the average reader.' He went ahead with it, anyway."

The rabbi then turned to me: "Mr. Wolfson, one of the most important qualities we look for in our future rabbis is honesty. You, my friend, are an honest person. We have no further questions. You are dismissed."

Shocked that Rabbi Greenberg had summarily called the interview to a halt after just ten minutes, I walked out of the room with Rabbi Brodie, who gently put his arm around my shoulder. "That was amazing, Ron," he chuckled. "We'll be talking about this for years. Stay here. The rabbis will deliberate, and I'll return with their answer." Five minutes later Rabbi Brodie returned. "*Mazal tov!*" he exclaimed. "Welcome to rabbinical school!"

An Educator, Maybe?

I still had a year to go before graduating college and moving on to the seminary. Meanwhile, like many prospective rabbis, I was teaching at a nearby synagogue, hoping to gain some experience and make a few dollars for movies and such. In my freshman year I took a job as a Kadimah youth advisor at Congregation B'nai Amoona, a Conservative synagogue headed by Rabbi Bernard Lipnick, a charismatic rabbi I had met through USY. When the cantor left the congregation on the second day of Sukkot in my sophomore year, I was pressed into service as a Bar/Bat Mitzvah tutor for forty-five— count 'em, forty-five!—Bar and Bat Mitzvah kids. Little did I know that what happened next would alter my career path.

One day Rabbi Lipnick called me into his office. "Ron, I've been thinking a lot about why kids hate Hebrew school but love summer camp." This immediately resonated with me.

"So I decided: why not do summer camp during the year? We should take the kids on *Shabbatonim*, Shabbat weekends during the year, maybe every month. We'll do it with the *vov* class, the sixth graders, after their Bar or Bat Mitzvah. Eighty percent of them are dropping out anyway, so what have we got to lose by trying something different from the same old Hebrew school with them? We'll make it voluntary; there will be extra cost the parents will need to cover. I need a young person, a youth leader type, to run the weekends and meet with the kids twice a week in between the retreats."

And then came the ominous rabbi voice: "I want you, Ron, to be that teacher."

I loved the idea. Why hadn't anyone else thought of this? It was the perfect answer to the problem of Hebrew school. The kids would love the weekends, especially those who go to summer camp. "I'll do it, Rabbi. I think it's brilliant!"

It was a disaster.

Well, the program was fine. My teaching was the disaster.

Classroom teaching is not the same as one-on-one tutoring. With a group, there are classroom management issues. I had no training whatsoever in how to control a classroom of hormone-driven, rambunctious fourteen-year-olds. And although I knew there would be twenty-three students, it was only on the first day that I learned that twenty were boys and only three girls. At four o'clock in the afternoon. On a Wednesday. This had "disaster" written all over it.

That first class was a complete *balagan* (zoo). The boys were out of control, the girls were intimidated, and I was bereft of strategies to gain their attention. My "nice guy" approach that worked so well in youth groups and Bar/Bat Mitzvah tutoring was useless, even counterproductive. The kids ran roughshod over me. I couldn't teach the lesson content; I couldn't get them to shut up. I couldn't do anything but reach back to a dark memory: "*Sheket!*" I screamed. "*Sheket, sheket, sheket!*"

Oh ... my ... God.

I was turning into Mr. Friedman. I fled the classroom in tears.

The next day I walked into Rabbi Lipnick's office, defeated, looking for help. He was compassionate and understanding. "Look, Ron, this dynamic would be tough for a veteran teacher. Why don't you go over to the School of Education at Washington U. and see if you can get some advice, maybe even take a course, read a book on classroom management. Give yourself a chance to learn some strategies. If need be, I'll come in and lay down the law. You'll be fine."

And that's exactly what I did. In the university bookstore, I found books that spoke to me: John Holt's *How Children Fail*, Neil Postman and Charles Weingartner's *Teaching as a Subversive Activity*.

There was a revolution underway in public education, a rejection of the strict discipline of the all-knowing, all-powerful teacher in favor of a "humanistic" approach to teaching, including discipline. I figured, if this is what was needed in secular education, all the more so in Jewish education. I devoured the books and developed my own strategy for working with the kids.

My classroom teaching improved rapidly and the weekends were a big success, enough that Rabbi Lipnick asked me to teach again the following year. This time I was ready.

At the orientation session I met the group of nine girls and six boys in the school wing of the synagogue the kids affectionately called "Banana Tuna" (because it rhymes with B'nai Amoona), standing at the door of the classroom, greeting each one with a simple "Hi, I'm Ron. What's your name?" Once everyone arrived, they sat in desks and waited for me to begin. I stood in front of the group and said, "Welcome! We're gonna do things differently in this class. Follow me!" and I began to walk out of the room, the kids trailing behind. I led them into the cavernous sanctuary and onto the bimah (pulpit), where I had set up a record player. I told the kids to sit in a circle on the floor of the pulpit and handed out a sheet of paper with the words to two songs.

"I want you to listen to these two songs, and then we'll talk about what they're trying to say." The kids were intrigued. This was different from Hebrew school. I put the first record on the turntable and played the song.

"Tradition! Tradition! ... Without our traditions our lives would be as shaky as ... as a fiddler on the roof!" The kids followed the words on the sheet; some of the girls sang along. And then the second song: "You say you want a revolution ..." All the kids sang the words of this, one of the most popular songs of the moment.

When the second song ended, I asked one question: "Okay, so what's the difference between 'Tradition' and 'Revolution'? What's *Fiddler* saying, and what are the Beatles saying?"

The kids jumped in, analyzing the texts, sharing their opinions. They talked not just with me, but with each other. I led the conversation to Judaism and the difficulties of changing a religious system. And then I lowered the boom: "Look, you guys, I don't know if you loved Hebrew school before your Bar or Bat Mitzvah or you hated Hebrew school. All I can tell you is that the *vov* class is gonna be different. We're gonna change our world. There will be no grades in this class. There is no book for this class; the themes you're interested in are what we will discuss, in class on Wednesdays and Sundays and on the weekends every month. What's on your mind? What do you want to talk about?"

It was the beginning of the most intense and exciting year of discovery for me, the foundational experience of my career as a Jewish educator. The mix of the formal setting of the classroom and the informal experiential educational environment of the weekend retreats afforded me the opportunity to experiment with teaching strategies, management techniques, and curricular development, all informed by my voracious reading of the general educational literature and fueled by my passion to do religious school differently. Rabbi Lipnick had given me carte blanche to figure it out, instinctively trusting that I would rise to the occasion.

What he didn't tell me until it was too late to jump ship was that he had decided to study the *vov* class as his long-delayed PhD in education dissertation project, sitting in the back of the classroom every weekend, taking copious notes on what transpired as an outside observer. I also took notes as the inside observer, a pioneering research methodology called "classroom microethnography" by Rabbi Lipnick's advisor at Washington University in St. Louis, Dr. Louis Smith. The opportunity to engage in what is today called "reflective practice"—the conscious recording of notes about not only what I planned to do in each session, but what actually happened—enabled me to grow exponentially as an educator.

By every measure, the 1970–71 *vov* class year was a spectacular success, so successful in creating a community in the classroom that the kids demanded to continue together for another year. The question remained: what would the purpose of a *zayin* (seventh-grade) class be? At the final banquet one of the kids casually tossed off a suggestion: "Why don't we all go to Israel together?" Rabbi Lipnick broke his yearlong silence to support the idea, and, suddenly, the kids had discovered a goal. As the parents picked up their teenagers at the conclusion of their final banquet, one of the kids yelled out, "Next year in Jerusalem!" echoing the eternal hope expressed at the Passover Seder.

Rabbi Lipnick, thrilled with the success of the *vov* class, immediately set about making arrangements for the kids to go to Israel the following summer. As for me, he had a new idea: "Ronnie, you are a born Jewish educator, I think one of the single best natural teachers I've ever known. As much as I know you would make a good rabbi, what we really need are great Jewish educators if we are to turn these schools around." He went on to propose that I do a longitudinal study of the *vov* class kids as they prepared for the trip to Israel, earning a PhD in education. It was an exciting opportunity—and I took it.

The summer in Israel was the most extraordinary educational experience of my life. If you were to search the shelf of doctoral dissertations at Washington University in St. Louis, you would find a 1,205-page, two-volume tome titled "A Description and Analysis of an Innovative Living Experience in Israel: The Dream and the Reality," written by Ronald G. Wolfson. That's me.

Unlike most visitors who view Israel through the windows of a hotel and a tour bus, the kids from B'nai Amoona lived with Israeli families in moshav Nir Galim for nine and a half weeks, worked the first four weeks in melon fields, celebrated Shabbat in a religious community, toured the country in the back of pickup trucks, and made lifelong friends. On the first day they were welcomed by the Israeli parental and teenage hosts as guests, but on the last day they departed as adopted daughters and sons, sisters and brothers. At the final banquet the director of the moshav addressed the community: "We have been calling these children '*Americayim*' all summer. They are not *Americayim*. They are *chaveirim* (friends)." The kids had been so successful at internalizing the norms of the Jewish culture of Nir Galim, they had transformed the somewhat negative connotation *Americayim* into *chaveirim*—members of the community. It was an incredible compliment.

You cannot imagine the scene on the final evening as we boarded the bus for Lod Airport—it was like the final good-byes at summer camp, times ten. Tears of joy at what had transpired, tears of sadness at separation, and many, many kisses. "Return to us soon!" the Israeli fathers cried. The mothers chased the bus down the road when we pulled out of the moshav, as if their own children were leaving for good. It was the ultimate in Jewish experiential education.

For Susie and me, it was not an easy summer. In addition to leading the group and counseling the American kids through the experience, I spent every private moment making notes on what was happening, going to bed late each night with a tape recorder in my hand. When we returned from Israel, I threw myself into the collected data to write the story and to analyze why it had been such a powerful summer. I holed away in a cubicle at the university library, emerging only for the St. Louis Blues hockey games—we had finally scored season tickets. Susie was busy teaching in a Title One program at a local elementary school. Somehow, though, we found time to get pregnant.

Novice teacher

Wrestling with God

We loved being pregnant. I say "we" because throughout the uneventful pregnancy, I felt as close to the baby-to-be as a father could. I marveled at every stage of development during the nine months, especially when the baby moved. A leg or an arm would push out from Susie's belly, seemingly anxious to come out and play. What an amazing feeling it is to touch a human being *in potentia* within the womb! Pregnancy is a time of great excitement and anticipation. Will it be a girl or boy? Will she or he look like Susie or me? What will we name the child? How will having a child change our lives? We had taken Lamaze childbirth classes and awaited the due date. The superstitions about setting up a nursery notwithstanding, we had ordered the basic furniture and bought a few toys. Our parents came to St. Louis in anticipation of the birth. We hadn't thought for even an instant about the possibility that something could go wrong, *terribly* wrong.

Our first child was born full term on the afternoon of May 6, 1974, and died thirteen hours later. The baby had become stressed during a prolonged labor, and Susie was rushed into an emergency cesarean section. Due to the stress, the baby had ingested contaminated amniotic fluid, a medical condition known as meconium aspiration. Despite the valiant efforts of a team of neonatal specialists throughout the night, there was no way to save her.

The baby had been rushed from the delivery room to the neonatal intensive care unit of Children's Hospital, across the street from Barnes Hospital, where Susie remained. The doctors and nurses were superb, bringing us updates on the baby's condition, but holding out little hope. At one point a social worker suggested I see the baby, a girl. It was a heart-wrenching moment, the helpless infant attached to monitors and tubes, her skin a dreadful blue instead of a bright pink. I spent most of the night crying, thinking about Susie and how devastating this loss would be for her.

Susie had spent the night recovering from the operation in the last room at the end of the hall on the maternity floor. The first inkling she had that something was wrong came when a nurse walked into the room and took down several decorative pictures of smiling mothers holding their newborns. I talked to her by phone, admitting that there was a problem, suggesting that she try to rest from the ordeal of the labor and operation.

Early in the morning a terrific young intern who had worked all night on the case came into the waiting room to give me the news, but his crying eliminated the need for words. The shock overwhelmed me, even though I knew it was coming. I literally ran across the street to the hospital wing where Susie had been taken. "She died" were the only words I could get out before collapsing into her arms. We cried together for a long time at this most unhappy ending. Little did I know that the ordeal had just begun.

No one knew how to handle this tragedy—no one. The nurses moved Susie from the maternity floor to the urology ward to save her the pain of hearing the sounds of babies. The obstetrician came by the room to say he was sorry and then informed us that because he had had to do a C-section, he would have to add $350 to his fee. Our parents, who had come to St. Louis expecting their first grandchild, eagerly awaiting their opportunity to become *bubbies* and *zaydies*, were in a state of shock. Our friends rushed to the hospital to offer comfort, but most only exacerbated the hurt with comments like "You're young," "You'll have other children," "It'll be okay." Well, it was definitely not okay.

When Rabbi Lipnick heard the news, he ran to the hospital. He did his best to console us, but we were completely unprepared for what happened next.

"What do we do now?" I cried to him.

"Ron, you know that according to Jewish law, if a baby doesn't survive thirty days there is no funeral, no shiva. The cantor will pick up the baby and have her buried at the B'nai Amoona cemetery," the rabbi said.

"Are you kidding me?" I sobbed. "No funeral! Like nothing happened?"

"This is what we do," the rabbi said, putting his arm around my shoulder, his eyes welling up with tears.

It felt like a robbery. How could a tradition that is so wise about the process of grief—seven days of intense mourning, then thirty days of less intensity, then eleven months—simply bury the unnamed child in an unmarked grave? What should have been a moment of supreme joy had become the ultimate nightmare. Instead of rejoicing as new parents, we were plunged into intense grieving.

For Susie the loss was overwhelming. She felt enormous sadness, anger, and pain. Despite the assurances of doctors and social workers that we would recover, Susie felt unheard and abandoned. I refused to mourn, a terrible mistake. "We'll start over. We'll get pregnant again. Let's look to the future." I wanted to move on, as if the whole thing was a bad dream. I spent sleepless nights worrying about Susie and dealing with questions of faith. Why did this happen? How could God let this innocent baby die?

After a week in the hospital, Susie was well enough to return to our apartment. We could barely look into the room set up as a nursery. The *zayin* class kids we had become so close to asked to come by to see us. They had no idea what to say; words seemed meaningless, empty. As much as our family and community rallied to support us, in the depths of the night we wrestled with God.

A week later I walked across the stage in the central courtyard of Washington University to receive my PhD degree, a bittersweet moment if ever there was one. My seven years in St. Louis were quite wonderful in so many ways, but I couldn't wait to get out of there and begin again.

L. A.

Shortly after my graduation from Washington U., Susie and I packed up our car and set off from St. Louis to Los Angeles. I had finally decided against the rabbinate in favor of Jewish education, but I needed to round out my Jewish studies. I had discovered a place called the University of Judaism in Los Angeles (now called American Jewish University), then the West Coast branch of the Jewish Theological Seminary of America, which offered a master's in Jewish studies.

As we drove west, I kept humming the theme song of the TV show *The Beverly Hillbillies*: "Californy is the place you ought to be.... Swimmin' pools, movie stars." L. A. Sunshine. Palm trees. Hollywood. Sounded good!

Ha! The University of Judaism (UJ) was located in the old Hollywood Athletic Club in the grungiest neighborhood, dotted with X-rated movie houses and deserted storefronts. On my first day there I walked past a movie theater showing a movie called *Bambi*—not the one about deer. In the next block I encountered a woman of the night, but it was nine o'clock in the morning.

I threw myself into summer school at the UJ, and Susie looked for work. She found it a few blocks away at Temple Emanuel Day School.

We liked Los Angeles. We didn't love it. The freeways were intimidating. It was challenging to make friends, so many people being transient. And yet I enjoyed my studies at the UJ with a small group of fellow students who had no idea I was a PhD until one day the mail room delivered the University Microfilms copy of my dissertation to our classroom. That's the way I wanted it—to be one of the gang.

We were still grieving over the death of our baby, each of us in our own way. My way was to focus on the future, to work toward getting pregnant again, a clever form of denial. Susie was understandably deeply depressed, her mourning unresolved. Only when she heard about a support group called AMEND—Aiding Mothers Experiencing Neonatal Death, which was sponsored by Stephen S. Wise Temple, one of the largest Reform synagogues in L. A.—did she find an avenue for coping with this terrible loss.

That first year went by quickly. Rabbi Lipnick was constantly in touch, planning for my return to B'nai Amoona. But as the saying goes: Man plans, God laughs.

When the dean of the Department of Education decided to make *aliyah* (that is, move to Israel), the UJ offered me the opportunity to teach, a kind of tryout. It went well. By the middle of the second year, they made me an offer I couldn't refuse: an appointment as assistant professor of education and director of the education program, beginning in the fall of 1976.

It turned out that not being a rabbi was a huge plus. The UJ was looking to broaden its offerings and diversify its all-rabbinic full-time faculty. And there were perks to the job: full medical insurance, pension benefits, and most important to me, it was a tenure-track position. There were plans to build a new campus on Mulholland Drive in the center of a growing and vibrant Jewish community. Moreover, and this tickled me endlessly, since the UJ was formally a branch of the seminary, I would be a de facto member of the Jewish Theological Seminary faculty. Me, "*Sheket*" Wolfson, on the faculty of one of the great academic Jewish institutions in the world!

Things were falling into place. Opportunity had knocked. All we needed now was our own little family, and we felt fortunate when Susie got pregnant in the spring of 1975. A kindly physician at the hospital in St. Louis had given us the name of a doctor: "When you get to Los Angeles, call Roger Freeman in Long Beach. He is one of the top ob-gyn specialists in high-risk pregnancies." Dr. Freeman skillfully guided us through the pregnancy with his rigorous protocol, and on January 29, 1976, our daughter was born. We named her Havi Michele, and she transformed our lives. Susie became the mother she was meant to be. Our parents became the grandparents they longed to be: "Bubbie and Zaydie W." and "Bubbie and Zaydie K." We were parents—and suddenly, virtually everything I had planned to do as a Jewish educator changed.

A Dress
for Shabbat

We were beyond excited to bring Havi home to our apartment on Hamel Road. A beautiful little girl, she captured our hearts from the moment we saw her. In fact I went a *bissle mishugeh* (a little crazy). Having grown up with two brothers and five boy cousins, I was thrilled to have a little girl. So on my way home from the university on a Friday afternoon just a week after Havi was born, I drove past the Stork Shop on La Cienega Boulevard and got a big idea—a really big idea. Our little Havaleh needed to have an appropriate dress for her first Shabbat dinner at home.

So I walked into the baby store and told the clerk, "I'm looking for a beautiful white dress." (White is the favored color of dress on Shabbat at summer camps and in Israel.) The clerk took me immediately to the back of the store, unlocked a cabinet, and pulled out the most spectacular white dress, the likes of which I had never seen in my life. "I'll take it," I said to her, satisfied that Susie would love it.

When I walked into our apartment with a big package tied with a red ribbon, Susie was preparing dinner in the kitchen.

"What's that?" Susie asked as she greeted me with a welcome kiss.

"It's a present for Havi!" I said, beaming with pride.

"Ahhhhhhh," Susie sighed. "That's the sweetest thing ever! What a father you are!"

Then she opened the box, looked inside, and yelled a *geshry* (scream) the likes of which I'd never heard in my life:

"Iyiyiyiyiyiyiyi! Ronnie! *What have you done!* Do you know what this is?"

"It's a beautiful white dress!" I said confidently as Susie pulled out of the package a long white gown, with little pearls along the hem, and a little bonnet to go over the baby's *kepeleh* (head).

"Ronnie! This isn't just a white dress!" Susie screamed. "*This is a christening gown! A baptismal dress!* Little Christian babies get sprinkled with water in this gown! I'm not putting our Jewish baby in this dress!"

I answered immediately, "Oh, yes you are! I just bought this dress for seventy-five dollars, it was on sale, there are no returns. *Put the baby in the dress!*"

Susie relented, and thus one of the most precious first photos of Havi we have is a Polaroid instant print of our *pitzkeleh* (little one), swimming in the long white christening dress, with the little bonnet over her *punim*, slumped in an infant seat, on top of our Shabbat table right next to the challah. We laughed and laughed about my innocent faux pas, telling our parents, family, and friends the hilarious story. My colleagues at the university loved the fact that I, a Jewish educator, had bought his daughter a baptismal outfit for his daughter's first Shabbat dinner. True story. All my stories are true—and here's the (faded) photo to prove it!

Havi in her Shabbat dress

It was only the first celebration of our renewed weekly family ritual. Oh, before Havi, Susie and I lit candles every Friday night. We ate challah every Friday night. We celebrated Shabbat with our friends and colleagues on many Friday nights. But after our tragic loss, after the agonizing months of hoping to get pregnant again, after the nerve-racking, high-risk, highly monitored pregnancy, there was a deep sense of gratitude. When your own child joins you at the Shabbat table, you truly feel like a family, a new family. And so every week we celebrated Shabbat with joy, and laughter, and love.

It took a dinner out in a pizza restaurant to understand the power of what was happening. It was a place called Micelli's, the kind of old-school Italian place with lots of trellises with little sparkly lights, red Naugahyde booths, and tables festooned with red-and-white checkered tablecloths. Havi was just shy of a year old. As we climbed into the booth, I noticed a lit red patio candle with a little white net, the kind used at a barbecue. The instant Havi saw the candle, you know what she did? She began to circle the candle three times, sweeping her hands in front of her eyes. I looked at Susie. She looked at me. We said the same thing at the same time: "She's a genius!" And then we marveled at what we had just witnessed. I mean, really? What would most one-year-olds do when spotting a candle? They would sing "Happy Birthday" or try to blow it out. Not our genius Havi! No, she began to bless the candle—in the pizza place—with the same choreography she had been witnessing every week as her parents lit Shabbat candles. She had learned a simple little lesson of Jewish life: candles are for blessing, not blowing. And she learned this lesson not in an early childhood center, not in a summer camp, not in a day school. She learned it in our home, at our table, from her mommy and daddy, who themselves had learned it from their moms and dads—and from Bubbie Ida and her scratchy Shabbat kisses.

"It's called 'modeling,' Ronnie," Susie, an early childhood educator, explained. "Havi is imitating what she has seen in our home. But you can only imitate what you see. The challenge will be to teach parents who didn't grow up with this how to do it, why you do it, and inspire them to do it."

This realization struck me like a bolt of lightning. Suddenly I understood something that literally transformed the course of my teaching for the next twenty years: *the family is the most powerful Jewish educational setting*. It is the experience of Jewish family life that creates warm Jewish memories and strong Jewish identity. We Jewish parents and grandparents are the most influential Jewish teachers our children and grandchildren will ever have.

On that day, in that pizza restaurant, I became a Jewish family educator. Two years later, on June 21, 1978, we welcomed our son Michael Louis into the world. Our own little family would become the laboratory for shaping a creative, joyous, and meaningful American Jewish life.

Michael and his big sister

Learning Laboratory

In addition to Shabbat, we embraced all the Jewish holidays in our little family. Susie brought her phenomenal creativity to each and every one of them, crafting wonderful experiences and memorable moments. We believed it would be these memories that would connect our children with us, with our family, and with Judaism itself.

It was amazing to see the holidays anew through the lens of our children. Hanukkah especially—a kids' holiday if there ever was one—brought home the truth that, ironically, it is Christmas that often ignites Jewish identity.

As a kid, I learned this life lesson during the height of the Christmas season in Omaha. There was not a place you could go that didn't announce the fact that Christmas was coming. From the daily countdown in the newspaper of "shopping days 'til Christmas" to the incessant commercials on television, the holiday was everywhere. Our block became a virtual wonderland of sparkling lights outlining homes and trees; the stores and malls featured Christmas displays and merchandise; even our public school was adorned with a huge Christmas tree in the front entrance. The strains of the haunting Christmas music—from "Silent Night" to "Little Drummer Boy"—filled the air. There was no escape.

For a little Jewish child, December was the first test of one's identity, the first realization that you were not like almost everybody else. How do you cope? What do you say to the clerk who wishes you a "Merry Christmas"? How do you play Joseph in the annual school Christmas pageant? What can you possibly do to stop yourself from humming "I'm Dreaming of a White Christmas"?

When I was a young boy, my mother thought she had the answer. She would outdo Christmas. This explains the decorations, the presents each and every night of the eight days, the stacks of latkes, the Hanukkah gelt (money). It seemed to work, especially when our Christian next-door neighbor, Mrs. Lamm, called to complain to my mother that I had been teasing her son Alan, "You only have Christmas for one day; we have Hanukkah for eight!"

The plan worked marvelously until one year the fifth night of Hanukkah coincided with Christmas Eve, a fact of which I had been well aware. After the lights had been lit, the presents given, and the latkes consumed, my mother confidently tucked me into bed, saying, "Well, Ronnie, wasn't Hanukkah wonderful tonight?"

"Yes, Mommy," I dutifully replied. "Mommy?"

"Yes, honey."

"Mommy, can we take down the Hanukkah things—just for tonight—so Santa Claus won't know we're Jewish?"

A plea for more presents? A rejection of my nascent Jewish identity? I think not. Looking back on it now, I believe it was a half-hearted wish not to be different, if just for one night.

Perhaps this explains my paranoia when our own children began to confront Christmas at a young age. December in Los Angeles is nothing compared to December in Omaha, and yet many families do decorate their houses with Christmas paraphernalia. One year we were driving through a part of town that seemed to have an unusual number of homes that were elaborately decorated for Christmas. "Oh, look at the pretty lights!" Michael exclaimed. "They're not pretty," I replied. Susie looked at me incredulously as if to say, "How can you say that? They *are* pretty." But as much as I hated to admit it, I felt threatened by the remark. Somehow my darkest fears that the majority culture would steal my children's Jewish identity led me to deny the perfectly obvious fact that Christmas lights are indeed pretty. Yet my fears seemed justified when Michael asked, "Can we have lights on our house too?"

Just then, Susie, a wise and wonderful parent, said one of the most brilliant things ever. She said, "No."

She continued, "Those families are Christians, and they are celebrating their holiday of Christmas. We are Jewish, and Christmas is not our holiday. It's sort of like when you went to Josh's birthday party. Remember how you felt? You wanted it to be your party, but it wasn't. Your birthday is coming soon. But you could still have fun at Josh's party, watching him open his presents and blowing out his candles. Well, these people are having a party called Christmas, but it's not our party. So, it wouldn't be right for us to put lights on our house."

The best part of Susie's brilliant answer was not her simple "no," although that was pretty good. We parents are so afraid to deny our children anything, to set boundaries, and yet isn't that one of our most important responsibilities? The best part of Susie's answer to Michael was what she did *not* say. She did not say, "Christmas is their holiday; Hanukkah is our holiday." She did not compare the two. Good thing, because Hanukkah can't hold a candle to Christmas. Besides, the answer to Christmas is not Hanukkah, a minor Jewish holiday. The Jewish answer to Christmas is Passover, Sukkot, Shavuot, Rosh Hashanah, Yom Kippur, Tu BiShvat, Yom Ha-Atzma'ut ... and, okay, Hanukkah. The Jewish answer to Christmas is Shabbat—every week! If we are to counteract what Rabbi Harold Schulweis called the "Santa claustrophobia" of the December season, it is through appreciating the beauty of Christmas as a detached observer of the holiday, while not accepting it as our own. It's not our own.

When we got home, I realized that the only person having problems with Christmas was me! Havi and Michael were taking everything in stride. If the argument Susie had developed made sense, then there was no reason not to acknowledge the beauty of Christmas decorations. There was a difference between allowing the kids to sit on Santa's knee, something we never did, and admiring the celebration of Christmas. It was the difference between appreciation and appropriation. So the next evening we piled the kids in the car and drove to a street in a neighboring community that the residents had turned into "Santa's Lane," complete with tremendous displays of Christmas decorations. We "oohed" and "aahed" at the houses, then went for ice cream.

The kids never asked to do it again.

Of course, there is the great joke about the old Jewish guy who plays Santa at the department store for a few extra bucks. A little Jewish boy begs his parents to let him sit on Santa's knee. They relent. As the child climbs onto his lap, the Jewish Santa bellows, "Ho! Ho! Ho! And what would you like for Christmas, little boy?" The boy looks up at the Santa and says, "Oh, Santa! I'm not Christmas. I'm Hanukkah!" The Jewish Santa puts his hand on the

Cowboy Michael (5) and Queen Esther (7) trick-or-treating before Shabbes, 1983

Cowboys Ronnie and Bobby, Purim in Nebraska, 1957

boy's head and whispers, "*Ah gezundt ahff dine kepeleh!*" (A blessing on your head!)

The kids did ask if they could trick-or-treat on Halloween, a holiday with roots in paganism that was then gaining popularity in America. Susie and I discussed it at length and decided it wasn't worth a battle; we had drawn the line at Christmas and Easter. We took the kids trick-or-treating on Halloween, unless the holiday fell on a Friday night, in which case we did the candy run before Shabbat candle lighting. Of course, in a perfect example of the mash-up of American and Jewish holiday observance, Havi insisted on dressing up as Queen Esther, while Michael dressed up as a cowboy, which sounded vaguely familiar to me.

As our kids entered Jewish preschool, Susie and I searched for creative ways to bring Judaism alive in our home. There were precious few resources; Pinterest was science fiction back then. For that matter, so was the Internet itself. No, the only way to share cool ideas was by word of mouth, a very inefficient way to stoke the fires of creativity.

One night while visiting with our friend Judy Bin-Nun, we lamented the lack of a resource for Jewish family celebration. "What if we did a magazine?" I asked. "It could have crafts, stories, and basic information about how to celebrate each holiday. It would be great fun to put together." I had created the Clejan Educational Resources Center at the university and thought it would be a great project for the center to sponsor. We decided to call it *Chicken Soup*, a title that conjured up the warmth of Jewish family life.

It was a blast. For six years, six times a year, Judy, Susie, and I sat and brainstormed fantastic ideas for Jewish family celebration in the home. Within a year we had ten thousand families receiving the magazine, printed on brown kraft paper, with our little chicken mascot on each cover. The success validated my view that educating the Jewish family was missing from the national agenda of Jewish education.

Our family was becoming a research-and-development center for Jewish family education. No one called it that in the early 1980s, but it was exactly what we were doing—exploring how to transform traditional forms like Shabbat dinners, sukkah meals, Simchat Torah parades, Purim shpiels, Tu BiShvat picnics, and Passover Seders into content-rich, creative, and memorable family learning experiences.

Susie brought her knowledge of early childhood education, and I plumbed the depths of Jewish ritual to surface engaging ways to give the holidays meaning. Above all, we both wanted our family celebrations to be warm, welcoming, and great fun for our kids, for our extended family and friends, and for us.

So when Havi resisted coming to the Shabbat table to sit with us, Susie had her craft a written invitation to her Cabbage Patch doll to join us. That did the trick! After we blessed Havi with the traditional parental blessings, Havi pretended to do the same for her doll. When Michael did not want to go to the synagogue on Shabbat morning, instead of dragging him there kicking and screaming, I dragged out our big set of wooden kindergarten blocks and challenged him to build a sanctuary. He did, complete with "pews" filled with Lego people and a holy ark holding a pretend Torah, which he then presided over as "rabbi," draping a Gucci scarf around his neck as a *tallit* (prayer shawl).

All this ritual in the home had its impact, giving the children a strong sense of Jewish identity. One Saturday night in November—the night we turn back the clocks when daylight savings time is over—just after celebrating *Havdalah* marking the end of Shabbat and the beginning of the new week, I walked deliberately around the house, changing the clocks back an hour. Michael, five years old, trailed behind me as I performed this little ritual, twisting the knobs on the alarm clock in the bedroom, on the microwave, pushing the buttons on the VCR machine—remember those? Suddenly I felt a tug at my pant leg. It was Michael, looking up at me with curiosity brimming in his eyes. "Daddy," he asked. "Do Christian people do this too?"

For Sukkot we borrowed traditions from our Omaha roots, building a "Midwestern sukkah" in our backyard. One of my own fondest childhood memories was cutting down cornstalks in a friendly farmer's field, stuffing them in my dad's car, and placing them on top of our sukkah for *s'chach*, the greenery that covers the roof of the booth. In Los Angeles, most use palm fronds for *s'chach*. In our desire both to start a family tradition and to be unique among the sukkot in our community, we bought cornstalks from a local farmers' market, along with bales of hay to decorate our sukkah. Susie invented a pumpkin soup served in an actual hollowed-out pumpkin and crafted a hanging "ornament" made up of cut-up New Year's cards. One year the kids and I slept all night in the sukkah on pool lounges in sleeping bags, until the morning dew drenched us awake. On Simchat Torah, we showed up at the synagogue to join the parade of Torah scrolls with a family banner we had constructed.

Our Passover Seder was forever transformed after experiencing creative Seders with friends; a "Bedouin Seder" in a family room that had been turned into a huge "tent," with bedsheets draped from one corner of the room to the center, all furniture removed except for one small coffee table with a Seder plate on it, and pillows for guests to recline upon while the telling of the Haggadah unfolded in song and story; a "magical Seder" in which the leader enthralled guests young and old by making the *afikoman* disappear—literally!—turning water into "blood," unleashing plastic frogs from what appeared to be a completely empty magician's box, raining hail (Ping-Pong balls) down on the table, causing the little ones—and the adults!—to scream with delight.

We took these ideas and added our own to shape our creative Seder nights. Susie created a "Pat the Bunny" Haggadah for the children at our table, a loose-leaf notebook of pages with grape-scented scratch 'n sniff stickers on *Kiddush* cups, Moses puppets, and word games. She embraced a "froggy" theme, fashioning an avocado into a bumpy-green-skinned frog centerpiece, surrounded by "bullrush babes in baskets"—a hard-boiled egg, sliced in half, a gefilte fishlet placed in the yolk hole, with a dab of horseradish on top—a kind of Jewish deviled egg. We searched for—and wrote—parody songs to punctuate the evening. We pitched a tent in the backyard one year and asked every guest to dress as a character from Jewish history and come prepared to tell their story. Our family Seders became so legendary that we were profiled in the *L. A. Times!*[*]

An opportunity to share what I was learning about empowering families came along one day in 1984 when I met Jules Porter, a well-known leader in the Los Angeles Jewish community. Jules was in line to become the international president of the Federation of Jewish Men's Clubs, an important group of congregational men's organizations that support the work of the Conservative Movement. Jules was looking for a project. I suggested a book and materials to teach the creative celebration of Shabbat dinner. I called it *The Art of Jewish Living: The Shabbat Seder.* Over the next six years we published three more books: *Passover, Hanukkah,* and *A Time to Mourn, a Time to Comfort,* teaching, empowering, and giving permission to make Judaism come alive in the home.

Singing with Cabbage Patch dolls at the Shabbat table

---

[*] Kurt Streeter, "Reliving the Seder Story, in Old Ways and New," April 19, 2014, *Los Angeles Times.*

Recipes for Memories

Fast-forward twenty years: Susie—I call her "the Martha Stewart of Jewish living," that is, before Martha went to jail!—collected all her creative celebration ideas into a family recipe cookbook. The title of the book is *Recipes for Memories*. It's not only a memoir, cookbook, and scrapbook. It is the story of our family.

When Susie finished this incredible project, she presented a copy to each of our kids at Hanukkah. Havi took one look at it and broke down in tears of memory and gratitude. Susie was worried about giving it to Michael; a hipster and rock music maven, he was not so into the Jewish thing. Holding the book in his hands, Michael flipped through the pages in amazement and said, "Wow! This is my life!" and proceeded to read every word on every page.

My favorite page in Susie's masterpiece is about matzah balls, a dumpling made from matzah meal (matzah is unleavened bread) and eggs. My mom—"Bubbie W"—made big, fluffy, soft matzah balls that float in a bowl of soup. Susie's dad—"Zaydie K"—made golf-ball-size hard matzah balls, "sinkers" that sank directly to the bottom of the bowl. Susie put both recipes and a photo of each grandparent on one page and titled it "Dueling Matzah Balls."

The next Passover, Susie, as always, sent Michael a care package of holiday foods and objects with the hope that it would encourage him to have some kind of celebration if he was not visiting us. The day after Seder, Michael called to thank his mother for the package. "Mom, it was great that you included the matzah ball mix. I actually had a few friends over, we had a little Seder, and I made some chicken soup and matzah balls—and I used your cookbook, Mom!"

I thought Susie was going to fall off her chair when she heard that! She could hardly contain her curiosity and asked two questions: "Which recipe did you use ... and how did they come out?"

Michael calmly replied, "Well, I was going for Bubbie, but they came out Zaydie!"

What a moment! In an instant, our worries about Michael's relationship to Judaism and family were ameliorated. He understood how important it was to Susie for him not only to accept the gifts in the package, but to use them on his own Jewish journey. And to use his mother's family cookbook validated the years of work Susie had invested, both in assembling the book and in shaping our family. And to connect himself with his Bubbie and Zaydie demonstrated continuity between the generations. And to report on the results of his matzah-ball-making experiment with sly humor reflected an underlying value in our family dynamic—the fuel of fun.

When the Whizin family made a legacy gift to the University of Judaism, the Whizin Center for the Jewish Future was established and quickly became the central address for growing the new field of Jewish family education. Serving as the director, and in my new position as vice president of the university, I gathered together outstanding pioneers in teaching Jewish families as faculty for an annual summer seminar that garnered national attention and more than 1,000 participants over the eighteen years of our work together.

Meanwhile, Susie was recruited by the Bureau of Jewish Education to create one of the first "Mommy and Me" programs in Los Angeles. She called it "Momaleh, Tatelah." The fortunate women who brought their toddlers to Susie's classroom discovered a world of wonderful, creative, and meaningful activities, both to foster the intellectual and social development of the children and to strengthen the parenting skills of the moms.

When the international Jewish women's group Hadassah came to me in search of a new initiative to engage young Jewish women, I suggested they base the effort on Susie's model. Together with our colleague Harlene Appelman, we created a curriculum for their *Al Galgalim* (Training Wheels) family education program, filled with creative holiday ideas and excellent content for crafting a Jewish environment in the home. We recruited the late great Debbie Friedman to compose original music for the program. It was a huge success for Hadassah.

One of my favorite lessons from Susie is her ability to build self-esteem. Quick to compliment and appreciate others, she taught her toddlers and their moms a song she used in her early childhood career:

> We're proud of you,
> So proud of you!
> We're very, very proud of you!
> We hope that *you* are proud of *you* ...
> We're very proud of you, _____ [insert the person's name].

I sing this song to my graduate students who, frankly, are often eager for the affirmation and the message that they too should take pride in their accomplishments. And of course whenever one of our family members does something wonderful, we sing it— loud and strong.

We sang it to our very special nephew Avi after his amazing Bar Mitzvah. When we received an invitation to the ceremony at Temple Israel in Omaha, we couldn't believe it! How could Avi, who had no ability to speak, lead the congregation in prayer? How could he recite from the Torah? How could he give the Bar Mitzvah speech?

When the big day arrived, the sanctuary was packed. Avi strode to the pulpit in his brand-new suit and awaited instructions from his incredible teachers. Rabbi Azriel explained that although Avi could not speak, he would lead the service by interpreting the prayers—with his art! Before singing the prayer thanking God for the blessings of creation, Avi walked to the middle of the pulpit and proudly held up a painting he had drawn depicting the creation of heaven and earth. Before the prayer recalling ancestors, Avi held up a poster he had made of his family tree. When it came time to read from the ancient scroll of the Torah, brother Aaron read while Avi followed along. For his Bar Mitzvah speech, Doug and Sara said, "If Avi could speak, this is what he would say: 'Thank you to all of you for coming to share in my big day. Mom and Dad, sorry I got you up early this morning, but I was so excited. Aaron and Naomi, I love you, no matter what. To all my family, I keep photos of you near my bed and look at them every night. Thank you to my teachers for helping me prepare for this day. And, now remember, say 'hi' to everyone like I do, hug everyone like I do, and love everyone like I do.'" There wasn't a dry eye in the place.

Then, when the last prayer was recited, a miracle happened! Avi said his first word: "Yesss!" We counted our blessings that day as Avi taught us the strength of a human soul to overcome a physical obstacle and reach a spiritual height.

DUELING MATZAH BALLS

Zadie K's Matzah Balls

2 T. oil
2 large eggs, beaten
1/2 c. matzah meal
1 t. salt
2 T. chicken broth
or water

Blend oil and eggs together. Add matzah meal and salt mixture to egg and oil mixture. Blend well. Then add broth or water and mix again. Cover bowl and place in refrigreater for 15-20 minutes. Now, take walnut size d amounts of the mixture and roll into smooth balls. Place them on a sheet of waxed paper for about a 1/2 hour. Meanwhile, bring a large pot of water to a boil. Add some salt. Turn down heat. Add the matzah balls and cover. cook 30-40 minutes.

Recipe makes about 6-8 chewy golf ball sized matzah balls.

Bubbie W's Matzah Balls

12 eggs
1 box matzah meal
3-4 T. chicken soup
3 chicken bouillon cubes

Bring some water to a boil in your largest stock pot. Meanwhile, beat eggs and salt together until frothy. Very slowly, add box of matzah meal less 3 T. When mixed add 3-4 T. of the fattiest or yellowest part of the chicken soup. Scoop mixture into stock pot with an ice cream scooper. Cover immediately. Turn down to medium and cook 50-55 minutes. DO NOT uncover while cooking.

Makes 12-15 light and fluffy tennis ball size matzah balls.

Zadie K, me, and Bubbie W

Fiddler Redux

As word spread of our work in Jewish family education, I was asked to speak about it in visits to synagogues as a scholar-in-residence and at national conferences. I called my talk "What's Happening to the Jewish Family?" and in order to hook the audience, I developed a strategy of singing a song in the first minutes of the speech. Of course the natural choice of song for a talk on the Jewish family was the opening scene of *Fiddler on the Roof.* I told the congregation the true story (all my stories are true) of when I was tapped to play Tevye in our USY production and how moved I was when the character introduces each member of the Jewish family in Anatevka, person by person, traditional role by traditional role: "A fiddler on the roof—sounds crazy, no? But in our little village of Anatevka you might say, each one of us is like a fiddler on the roof, trying to scratch out a simple pleasant tune, without breaking his neck. It isn't easy ... but one thing helps us keep our balance—tradition!"

And then I burst into song, singing about papas who scramble day and night for a living, mamas who know how to make a quiet and kosher home, daughters who are taught to mend, tend, and fix, and sons who learn a trade at age ten. I hammed it up, encouraging the audience to sing the chorus—"The papas!"—while I sang the words to each verse. This came as a delightful surprise; no other speaker sang a song in their lecture. All those years of performing for Zaydie and the family in front of his big-screen TV and my subsequent musical comedy experiences in high school were paying off.

When we had finished the song, I unpacked the verses and contrasted the "traditional" role of each member of the Jewish family of the late nineteenth century with the Jewish family one hundred years later: "Today's papa—he still must scramble day and night to make a living, to feed his wife and children, but he rarely says his daily prayers, and it's highly questionable whether he has the right as 'master of the house' to have the final word at home! No, today's mama might be a homemaker, but more likely she is pursuing a career that was unimaginable in Golde's day, and no way is she running the home 'so papa's free to read the Holy Book.' She expects papa to chip in as a partner in homemaking, since she is working outside the house. Our daughters? Oh, my word. They have no time to learn how to 'mend, tend, and fix.' No, they are busy in science class and political science class, preparing to become doctors and lawyers, professions that Tzeitel, Hodel, and Chava could never have dreamed possible. Our sons? Well, maybe they start Hebrew school at three—if there's a good Jewish preschool available, they should!—but learn a trade at ten? I don't think so. And parents picking a bride for him? Not a chance."

With this introduction, I was off and running, outlining the substantial challenges facing Jewish parents as they navigate the raising of a Jewish family. I had learned from my rabbi Harold M. Schulweis to always end a talk with a "therefore": therefore, here is the action plan moving forward. I emphasized that so much of Jewish education is focused on children that we spend little time equipping parents and grandparents with the knowledge and skills required to be the role models of Jewish living in the home. I challenged the empty nesters in the audience: "Are you still lighting Shabbat candles? Are you still sitting in a sukkah? Because if you're not, then the message to your children was 'This is for you, not for me.' We adults must own Jewish living for ourselves. To do that, we must come to the synagogue for family education, to learn the hows and whys of Jewish practice so we can take our rightful place as the most important Jewish teachers our children and grandchildren will ever have."

The climax of my lecture was a surprising analogy, although perhaps a foreshadowing of my destiny as a one-hundred-thousand-miles-per-year frequent flyer: "You know, I'm always struck by something the flight attendants say during the safety demonstration at the beginning of a trip. They tell you what will happen if the air pressure escapes the cabin. Those little oxygen masks are released from the overhead panel. And then they give an instruction that is so counterintuitive, so surprising, that it always takes my breath away: 'If you're traveling with a child, put your mask on first and then help the child.'

"Sure. Right. You mean to tell me you're traveling with your child or your grandchild, there is a crisis on the plane, the air is escaping the cabin, the little orange masks come flying out of the ceiling, and you reach for your mask first? No way! If it were me, every bone in my body, every instinct I have is to get that mask on my child first. So why do they tell you to put your mask on first before helping the child? Because they know that if the oxygen is not flowing to you, the adult, you cannot help the child; you'll pass out first. And something else. The child needs to see you, the adult, *modeling* the behavior that can save a life. If we are to save our Jewish lives, if we are serious about Jewish continuity, then we better get the oxygen of Jewish living flowing to us, the parents and grandparents, first, and then we will be able to help our children and grandchildren be Jewish. Our friend Tevye would expect nothing less."

The message was well received. Word spread that this young professor of education was a good speaker—entertaining even. Requests from synagogues for me to be their scholar-in-residence began to pour in, and once again, as I had during my senior year of high school as USY regional president, I hit the road. Over the years I have spoken at innumerable conferences and visited hundreds of synagogues, Jewish community centers, schools, Federations, Hillels, women's groups, and summer camps across the United States of America, in Canada, Europe, Russia, South America, Israel, Australia, Hong Kong, New Zealand, and throughout the world. I stand in the lobby or at the entrance of the sanctuary or lecture hall and greet people with a simple "Hi, I'm Ron." I tell my true stories and I try my best to inspire young and old alike to embrace a Judaism of joy and laughter, of meaning and purpose, of belonging and blessing. What is important to me is not the talking, but the doing. Education is only as good as what it inspires us to achieve—stronger families, compelling sacred communities, individual Jewish journeys that change us, that make a difference, that empower us to be better human beings, reflections of the divine image. This is why I tell my true stories. This is why I love being a teacher.

Why Doesn't Everyone
Love Synagogues?

I learned how to be Jewish in two places—my family and my synagogue. I was a shul kid.

I assumed that everyone loved shul as much as I did. Only when I got older did I realize ... ummm ... not so much. Actually, there are a lot of reasons people don't come to synagogue. Some consider the worship services too long or boring. Some have had bad experiences visiting synagogues, as when no one says hello. Some are afraid they will be asked to do something they do not know how to do, such as wrap the Torah or recite a blessing. When I put myself in the shoes of the Jews in the pews who don't love shul, I began to understand how really intimidating a synagogue can be. If there has been any value-added piece to my work in synagogue life, it is that I am not, nor have I ever been, a rabbi. I sit in the congregation, just like a member or guest. I have done my own personal "pew study."

I wish I had a nickel for every time someone told me of their experience visiting a synagogue for the first time such as this: A woman in a state that begins with the letter "O" and a city that begins with the letter "C" tells me, "I went shul shopping in this town, and in the first three places I visited, no one said hello." Another woman in the same state, but a different letter "C" city says, "I've belonged to this Reform temple for five years." I ask, "How's it going?" She says, "Oh, I love my rabbi"—that's the best compliment ever for a rabbi—"but I can't break into the cliques in the congregation." I myself visited a synagogue in a city that starts with the letter "B" in a state with the letters "MD" and I walked around the building for a good twenty minutes before someone greeted me. His name was Winston. How did I know his name was Winston? He was the custodian, the only one wearing a name tag.

And then one Shabbat morning in a large Conservative congregation in a state that begins with a "P" in a city that begins with a "Ph," I experienced firsthand what many newcomers have encountered on their first visit to a synagogue. I had been invited as scholar-in-residence to speak on Friday evening. After I gave my talk, the rabbi emeritus, a longtime acquaintance, said, "Ron, they won't make you sit on the bimah tomorrow morning. Would you like to sit with me?" I readily agreed.

The next morning, I showed up promptly at 8:55 a.m., five minutes before the start of the Shabbat morning service. As I looked around the enormous sanctuary—the kind that sleeps eight hundred—I saw about eight people in the room: the *shames* (synagogue caretaker), four or five regulars, who I assume always come on time, and three guests of that day's Bat Mitzvah who had taken the invitation time literally! They didn't know you could show up at 10:30 a.m. Then the service began, but still no rabbi emeritus was in sight.

I took a seat on the aisle one row from the back of the sanctuary, hoping to see the rabbi when he came in. About ten minutes passed and I felt a tap on my shoulder. I looked up and saw a sweet older man looking at me with the saddest eyes. He said, "You know, I wouldn't tell you that you are sitting in my seat"—he then pointed to an empty seat directly behind me in the last row—"and I would sit there," he continued, "but if I sat there, where would my friend who always sits there sit?" I looked around. There were 785 empty seats! But this man needed the seat I was in.

Of course I moved immediately because I knew that man. Not *personally*, but I knew his type. That man was a regular who had been sitting in that seat for fifty years. In a way, his need to sit in that seat is one of the great things about being a member of a sacred community. There is even a name for it in Jewish tradition: *makom kavu'a,* his "fixed place" in the congregation. And it is true that if his friend who sits behind him is not in his usual seat, then the friends who know him would be worried: is he sick? So I found another seat, and he took his.

At the *Kiddush* lunch afterward, his friends who witnessed this incident really lit into him. Why? Because he kicked the *scholar-in-residence* out of his seat! If I had been a stranger, or someone looking for a congregation, or a guest of the Bat Mitzvah, it would have been no big deal. Eventually the rabbi emeritus showed up, but the experience taught me a lesson.

What could that man have said that would have gotten him his seat *and* welcomed me to the synagogue? No, not "Would you like to sit somewhere else?" The first thing that should have come out of his mouth was "*Shabbat shalom!*" He knew I was a stranger. And then "Would you like to sit with me?" I would have loved that; I would have moved over, he would have his seat, and I would have made a new friend.

I learned something else during my travels to synagogues. Sometimes people are inadvertently embarrassed despite our best intentions.

This came home to me big-time at another Conservative synagogue where the rabbi insisted I sit on the pulpit during the service. On this particular Saturday morning there was a big Bar Mitzvah that brought in a large crowd. When it came time for the Torah reading, the family members who were to receive the honor of reciting the blessings over each portion were escorted to the front row of the sanctuary. The guy sitting in the fifth seat was clearly nervous, clutching a small card and staring at it like his life depended on it. Of course, on the card were the Hebrew blessings he was about to chant in front of his family, friends, and six hundred complete strangers. He was a tall, handsome man, elegantly dressed in what looked to be a hand-tailored suit. Later I learned this guy, let's call him "Number 5," was one of the most powerful and successful attorneys in the community. But at that moment he looked like a nervous patient awaiting a tooth extraction.

Clutching the little card for dear life, Number 5 was rehearsing the unfamiliar Hebrew of the Torah blessings until it was his turn to take his place in the "on-deck circle," a big overstuffed chair on the far side of the pulpit. When Number 4 came up to bat, standing at the side of the Torah reading table, ably reciting the blessings, I looked over to see how Number 5 was doing. He looked sweaty, fidgeting with his *tallit*.

As in most traditional synagogues, there was one person choreographing the Torah service, a lovely gentleman who is known as a *gabbai*. Clearly, the *gabbai* in this shul knew that many of the Bar/Bat Mitzvah family members given the honor of chanting the blessings had little or no idea what to do when approaching the reading table. So he was giving stage directions under his breath, thinking no one could hear him: "Go here, stand there ..." the *gabbai* whispered. But there was an excellent sound system in the sanctuary, so everyone heard all of his instructions.

It was Number 5's turn. I suspected he had not been in a synagogue since his own Bar Mitzvah, if he had one at all. I mean, the guy didn't know a Torah from a hora (an Israeli dance), if you get my drift. The look on his face as he walked up to the reading table was one of sheer terror; the poor man was *shvitzing* like an NBA basketball player mid-game.

The *gabbai* saw that Number 5 had no clue what to do, so he whispered the following instruction, thinking no one could hear, but everyone heard: "Grab your *tallis** ... and kiss your *tzitzis***!"

Number 5 turned white. All the blood rushed from his face. Horrified and confused, he whispered back, thinking no one in the congregation would hear, but of course, everyone could: "Kiss my *what?!*"

The single funniest—and saddest—thing I ever witnessed in a synagogue. This man was smart, used to being in control, confident

---

* *Tallis* is Yiddish for *tallit*, prayer shawl.

** *Tzitzis* is Yiddish for *tzitzit*, the four fringes on the corners of the *tallit*.

with what he's doing, but his experience on the bimah was infantilizing and embarrassing. Do you think he'll be back in the synagogue anytime soon?

Synagogues would be well served to ensure that every guest, every relative of the Bar/Bat Mitzvah, every member who only shows up occasionally is not only welcomed warmly, but also sensitively prepared for the worship experience.

A Vision for
Transforming Synagogues

These experiences weighed on me, and when Rabbi Rachel Cowan offered a planning grant from the Nathan Cumings Foundation for a project on synagogues, she asked me to consult with her rabbi, Larry Hoffman. I knew of Lawrence A. Hoffman, a professor of liturgy at Hebrew Union College–Jewish Institute of Religion in New York, and had read his groundbreaking book *The Art of Public Prayer*. What I didn't know until I spoke with him was that Larry had become a leading voice for the transformation of worship in the Reform movement, influencing a generation of rabbinical and cantorial students as one of the most beloved teachers at the college.

On that first phone call, Larry and I discovered that we were both scheduled to be at a food-laden Rabbinical Assembly convention in the Catskill Mountains, where he had been invited to give a keynote address and I was offering a workshop on family education to one of my primary audiences in the Conservative movement. We decided to meet, neither of us having great expectations. But after what seemed like hours of animated conversation, we realized that we shared much of the same love for and critique of synagogue life and a passion to do something about it. We quickly ascertained that because of our relative standings within our movements, we could create a project that would speak to 90 percent of North American synagogues. We reveled in the fact that Larry was a rabbi and I was a Jewish educator, each bringing different skills and knowledge to the effort. He lived on the East Coast, while I lived on the West Coast. He was raised in a small town in Canada, while I grew up in a small town in the Midwest. He could not sit still while he talked, and neither could I. We left the meeting promising each other to become partners in planning this as-yet-unnamed project to deepen synagogues.

We called our project Synagogue 2000. We gathered the best of the best clergy, consultants, and artists to envision the synagogue of the twenty-first century. Our conferences—we called them "glimpses of the Emerald City"—were spectacular laboratories for cutting-edge worship, community building, and learning. We produced two sold-out "*Hallelu* celebrations" of synagogue life—one at the Universal Amphitheatre in Los Angeles and one at the Fox Theatre in Atlanta—featuring the top musical artists in the Jewish world—Debbie Friedman, Theodore Bikel, Neshama Carlebach, Alberto Mizrahi, all organized by Craig Taubman. I suggested we not sell individual tickets to the public, but rather sell blocks to synagogues so when the members came to the venue, they all sat together, like state delegations at a national political convention. The music was spectacular, uplifting; the people were dancing in the aisles. A highlight came near the end when Larry and I asked all the clergy and staff of the synagogues to rise from their seats: "You are always blessing us at the key moments of our lives," I proclaimed. "Today, we will bless you and thank you for all you do to bring us a Judaism of meaning, purpose, and celebration." And then the thousands of laypeople recited the ancient priestly benediction over the synagogue professionals, many of whom were moved to tears.

We created a Synagogue Studies Institute that commissioned research about synagogue life, documented in a series of "S3K Reports."* We published graduate-level curricula for synagogue teams to reflect on their efforts to engage people in community, the worship experience, family education, and healing. Larry wrote

---

* By then, we'd changed the name to Synagogue 3000.

Rethinking Synagogues and I wrote *The Spirituality of Welcoming* and
Relational Judaism (all Jewish Lights Publishing) based on our work.
We studied independent minyanim (worship groups) and stimu-
lated efforts in synagogues to reach young Jewish professionals in
our Next *Dor* project. It was a marvelous twenty-year collaboration
that changed the conversation about synagogue life in North
America and made a significant difference in how synagogues create sacred communities of meaning and purpose, belonging and
blessing.

Much of what I know about transforming synagogues comes from
my experiences in church. When we launched Synagogue 2000,
Rabbi Elie Kaplan Spitz, a colleague who had read about our project, suggested that I visit Saddleback Church. It was becoming a
"megachurch," defined as a congregation that attracts five thousand or more people for a weekend service. The pastor, Rick Warren, had come to Orange County, California, knocked on doors
in the affluent neighborhood of Lake Forest, and asked a simple
question: "Do you go to church?" If the answer was yes, he said,
"God bless you," and walked on. If the answer was no, he asked
why. The answers he heard—the sermons are boring; the music
is old-fashioned; I don't want to get dressed up; all they want is
my money; I can't trust the child care—ignited a passion in Rick
to create a church that would be the exact opposite experience:
a message of personal empowerment that people could hear on
Sunday and use on Monday; great soft-rock music; a "contribute-
what-you-want-when-you-want" ethos; an outstanding religious
school; and a "come-as-you-are" dress code. Rick himself showed
up at services wearing Hawaiian shirts and sneakers. He called Saddleback a "seeker-sensitive church," an evangelical place designed
to engage those who shied away from religion.

The first time I met Rick, I knew he was something special.
"Ron, come here, you!" he shouted, embracing me in a huge bear
hug. "Have you hugged a pastor lately? I hope you don't mind!

Elie has told me all about you and your synagogue project. How can I help?"

"Great to meet you, Rick," I responded. "I'd like to bring my partner Larry Hoffman to Saddleback for services, and then we would love to bring a couple of busloads of synagogue leaders from sixteen congregations across the country for a Sunday afternoon service."

"Well, sure," Rick enthused. "We can arrange that. It'll be fun to see what y'all think about our place."

Here's what I think about Saddleback Church: It's amazing. There is so much a synagogue can learn about how to build a welcoming congregation that I take my graduate students in education and rabbinical school for a site visit to Saddleback every semester. Rick has become a good friend, always willing to share his knowledge with the Jewish community. He's a mensch, and I feel honored to call him a friend, even though we disagree about very important issues. But as Rick likes to say, "You don't have to see eye to eye to walk hand in hand."

Mrs. Maizie

While I was busy at the university and with my projects, Susie concluded that her part-time wages as a preschool educator and my salary as a professor would not pay for our children's education. So as the day school tuitions mounted, Susie decided to take a break from her early childhood teaching and go into business. The question was, what business?

On a visit to Omaha, we discovered it. Susie knew that my favorite treat was great popcorn, prepared a certain way, a way I had learned as a child: small white kernels popped in corn oil. I often remarked that Orville Redenbacher had foisted a canard on America, insisting that the bigger the kernel, the better the popcorn. Untrue. The sweetest, tastiest popcorn came from small gourmet seeds. And by popping the corn in pure corn oil, the flavor of the popcorn was that of corn, through and through. (Though Mrs. Yawel's coconut oil popcorn was pretty good too!)

On that day in Omaha we learned that a local company had begun to market just such a corn-on-corn prepopped popcorn in the supermarkets. There was nothing like it in California. When we returned to Los Angeles, Susie developed recipes for a gourmet white popcorn in regular, low-salt, and no-salt varieties, a white cheddar cheese, and a caramel corn. She designed an upscale bag with a window for customers to see the product and hired an artist to create a logo. She found a commercial corn popper in Los Angeles who agreed to pop and pack the corn to her specifications. She

134

named the brand "Maizie's Gourmet Popcorn," a riff on the Spanish word for corn, *maize.*

With virtually no capital, no distributor, and no marketing budget, Susie began her business by presenting the popcorn in a few local convenience stores. Donning a kitchen apron emblazoned with her logo, she would set up a card table in a high-traffic spot in the grocery store to demonstrate her product, doling out samples of each variety. An indefatigable saleswoman, Susie would not let a single person walk by without trying her delicious popcorn. People loved it, thrilled that it was a local product and excited to meet the creator herself. She called herself "Mrs. Maizie," schlepping cases of popcorn in her station wagon all across Los Angeles.

Maizie's took off. Within a year Susie had secured distribution in seven hundred Vons stores and a number of smaller chains. It took two years to get space in Gelson's, the top-of-the-line upscale market, but once on the shelves, Maizie's flew off them. Typically a demonstrator will go through two or three cases of product in a day of sampling. Susie would triple that number. Sales went through the roof, and Maizie's Gourmet Popcorn became the number-one-selling snack food in Southern California.

When the big players like Frito-Lay and Granny Goose entered the category with their huge marketing clout, Susie sold Maizie's to a Midwestern popcorn company, Vic's. She had built a fantastic business in a tough, male-dominated competitive environment. Like Mrs. Yawel, the popcorn lady at Zaydie Louie's bar, Susie's

Mrs. Maize

success put our kids through day school and university and brought her enormous well-earned respect from friends and family, especially my entrepreneurial mom. Three extraordinary women in my life succeeded in the rough and tumble world of business.

Life Lesson at AAA

Havi decided to attend the University of Michigan for college. That fall we arranged to be in Omaha for Rosh Hashanah with the family and planned to rent a car and drive Havi to Ann Arbor. But I had no idea how to get there.

I belong to AAA, the American Automobile Association. I carry my AAA membership card in my wallet. It says I've been a member for forty-two years. In all that time I have used the card for roadside services only twice—once when I had a flat tire and once when the car battery died. When I needed a map to Michigan, I remembered my AAA card and went into the local office in Omaha, an experience that became a metaphor for much of my teaching about Jewish living.

I was warmly greeted at a reception desk. I showed my membership card to the receptionist and asked for a map from Omaha to Ann Arbor.

"Well," the receptionist said, "we can certainly get you a map, but wouldn't you like to meet with someone and really plan your trip?"

I was in no particular hurry and agreed. Within minutes, I was escorted to a counter and introduced to Steve, my personal counselor. "Hi. I'm Steve, how can I help you?"

"I'm going from Omaha to Ann Arbor ..."

"Great," Steve replied, and he pulled out a huge map of the United States of America and used a yellow marker to highlight a path from Omaha to Ann Arbor. This gave me the big picture of the journey.

"Thanks," I said and prepared to leave with my map.

"Wait a second," he stopped me. "Let me show you this."

Steve then pulled out a map of the Central States Region and began the same drill, marking a route from Omaha to Ann Arbor with that little yellow marker. I noticed this map had more detail than the first one.

"Thanks," I said, and prepared to leave with my second map.

Oh no. Steve had something else up his sleeve.

"Now that we have an overview," Steve smiled, "I'm going to make you a TripTik."

"A what?" I asked.

Steve began to pull together a whole series of small strip maps of the route he had outlined on the large map and the regional map. Each strip map showed at most 150 miles between points along the way.

The TripTik maps were very different from the larger maps of the United States; there was much more information. There were notes about the terrain ("soft, rolling fields of corn becoming grazing for livestock in the east"). On the back there were even brief descriptions of points of interest along the way.

I noticed that just south of Des Moines, Iowa, the road led to Madison County. I couldn't help but ask Steve, "Is that *the* Madison County?"

"Yep," Steve laughed. "My wife made me read that book too!"

"Can you actually visit the bridges of Madison County?"

"Yep. My wife dragged me there a couple of years ago. They are actually really romantic. My wife loved them. If you have time, you should stop there. Want a map?"

Steve continued through my itinerary, pulling out map after map, and then to top it all off, he produced two thick tour books, the kind with the descriptions of sites, listings of accommodations, and things to do on the journey. By the time our forty-five-minute consultation was over, I had a sack full of maps, tour books, and my personalized TripTik. I left the AAA office feeling excited and confident about taking the journey.

Call me contrarian or old school, but I love the TripTik far more than the GPS on my smartphone. I suppose they are getting to be more accurate, but I simply don't trust the GPS. I once heard a report on NPR about a group of tourists who used their GPS to navigate their way out of Bryce Canyon toward the Grand Canyon but ended up on nearly impassable dirt roads that led to a sheer cliff. The chief deputy of the Utah highway patrol told the *Salt Lake Tribune* that a GPS device is "no substitute for good judgment or detailed topographical maps. People can start down a nice, graded dirt road and it can soon turn into boulders and deep washes, but they continue driving instead of turning around. I don't understand it. The shortest way is not always the quickest way."*

On the way back to Omaha from Ann Arbor, Susie and I did visit the famous bridges of Madison County. Very romantic. Many kisses. We had the best time that night in the Motel 6. That guy, Tom Bodet, left the light on for us.

True story. All my stories are true.

---

* Mark Haynes, "Trusting GPS, Convoy of Visitors Get Monumentally Lost," *Salt Lake Tribune,* August 5, 2008.

What Do I Do
Till the Kids Say "I Do"?

This was the great title of a book I could write about the period of our lives when we were dreaming and scheming to get Havi married after she graduated Michigan. I think many parents agonize over the quality of the people their daughters bring home. Havi had her share of relationships that we celebrated and a few that worried us mightily. Once she flew our coop, the people she met were out of our hands. That didn't stop us from scouring the sanctuary during Rosh Hashanah services for potential mates. That didn't stop me from announcing to a convention of Hadassah ladies, "I have a beautiful twenty-six-year-old daughter; anybody have a nice guy for her?" and then passing around her glamour shot. We colluded with our best friends to set up their sons with Havi, but, alas, such a suggestion from parents to adult children is usually the kiss of death. Why this craziness? Certainly we cannot imagine our kids living life alone. But it also comes from a deep-seated desire for the continuity of generations.

Thank goodness for girlfriends. After Havi returned to Los Angeles to enroll in social work graduate school, a girlfriend suggested she get on JDate, a popular Internet Jewish dating site. At first Havi didn't want anything to do with it, but once she got on the site, she was like a kid in a candy store. She would troll through the profiles of guys, email them, and set up coffee dates. Often she would have six JDates a night at Starbucks and come home to report to us, bouncing off the walls from the caffeine. One night she came over and said, "I found him! He's perfect on paper!"

"What means 'perfect on paper?'" I asked.

"He's thirty-two, tall, handsome, on his JDate profile he has his arm around his Bubbie, he goes to shul ... and he's a dentist!" Havi enthusiastically reported.

Turns out the dentist fell for Havi right away too. The instant he saw this beautiful young lady, he said, "Forget coffee. We're going for dinner." In the JDate world, this is known as an instant upgrade.

Havi and the dentist quickly became attached. He had real potential. Things looked very, very promising. He was charming, paid for everything, and even took Havi to his synagogue for services. Gifts were exchanged, the parents met, and the dentist became a fixture in our home. Month after month went by and we began to ask Havi, "So, *nu?* When will he ask you to marry him?" We were convinced the engagement was around the corner, and being the sentimentalists we are, we hoped he would ask for our blessing. Well, they dated for six months, a year, a year and a half—nothing. Young people today certainly take their time.

Mit'n drinen (in the middle of all this), my university changed its dental plan. At a Friday night Shabbat dinner in our home, I mentioned it to the dentist. He offered to take care of me. I was all over that. I went, he was pretty good, and best of all, he charged the family rate. I came home and said to Susie, "You gotta go!"

Susie freaked out. "No way! I don't want him putting his hands in my mouth," she said. "Too weird."

"Honey," I protested, "this guy could be our son-in-law. You've got to go!"

Eventually, Susie gave in. I'll never forget what she said as she got into her car for the first appointment: "Good thing he's not a gynecologist!"

Susie returned from the dentist's office with an even better story. "How'd it go?" I asked.

"Oh, he was fine," Susie said. "But you know how when you go to a new doctor's office for the first time, they give you a form to fill out with all your demographic information?"

"Yeah," I said.

"Well, the receptionist gave me a clipboard with the form on it. I sat down and looked at it. The first line asked for 'Name.' So, I wrote in 'Susan Wolfson.' The second line on the form was 'Name I Prefer to Be Called.'" I wrote in '*Mom*'!"

The good DDS never noticed it, or pretended not to; he never said a word. We should have known it was a sign.

One night the phone rang. "Mom, Dad!" It was Havi. "We're in Hawaii ... and we're engaged! *Mazal tov!*"

He never asked us for our blessing—and that should have been a sign too.

Havi showed us the engagement ring; it was not the diamond they had picked out together. "He got a better deal on this one," Havi mumbled.

It went downhill from there. The dentist turned out not to be the guy we all thought he was. Six weeks before the wedding, Havi did one of the most courageous acts imaginable—she broke off the engagement. We were relieved. She saved her life. Oh, there was a mourning period. She was sad that her dream wedding and dreams of a new life had dissolved. But two of Susie's girlfriends told Havi that they had gone down the aisle knowing he was the wrong guy—and they lived to regret it.

Two years later she met a guy named Dave. He was working for a small Internet company called Google. Once again Susie and I waited out the courtship. In the middle of their second year of dating, my father-in-law Abe came to Los Angeles to visit. Havi had not moved into Dave's Long Beach Marina condo, but she put on a beautiful Shabbat dinner at his place. After a lovely meal, Abe pushed his dishes to the middle of the table, looked at Dave, and blurted out, "So, *nu?* Vat's the holdup?" Dave handled the question magnificently. "Oh, Zaydie," he began, wisely referring to Abe as if he were already his grandfather-by-marriage, "you know I love your granddaughter and we're heading in the right direction. Hang on!"

"Vell, I'm not getting any younger," ninety-eight-year-old Abe reminded them.

One day Dave called us. He wanted to come over to visit—without Havi. When he walked into the house, he was clearly nervous. We sat on the living room couch. I wanted to kibitz about Google, but he had come for one purpose.

"Listen, Ron and Susie," he began. "I love your daughter more than anyone or anything in the whole world. And I would love your blessing to spend the rest of my life with her."

I just started to cry. I stood up, gave him a hug and a kiss on the cheek, and said, "Welcome to the family!"

Can you imagine our joy when Havi gave birth to our first grandchild, a girl, named "Ellie Brooklyn?" Why "Brooklyn"?

Well, my father, may he rest in peace, was from Brooklyn. Dave's mom is from Brooklyn. They needed a "B" to honor the memory of my mom, Bernice, may she rest in peace. And Brooklyn is a hot place right now.

The next day I called Larry Hoffman in New York City to share the good news. "I have a new granddaughter! Her name is 'Ellie Brooklyn.'" I mused.

Larry did not hesitate. "Ron, you're gonna have four more grandchildren—Manhattan, Staten, Queens, and if you have a boy, you can call him 'The Bronx'!"

The kids did have a boy all right; our grandson arrived two years later, but they named him "Gabriel Elijah." As the Zaydie, I was honored to be the *sandak* (companion of the child, a godfather) at the bris eight days later.

This was a huge moment for me. Holding a boy in my arms during this ancient rite of relationship brought home the continuity of the generations of our Jewish family. I wondered if my Zaydie Louie had held me during my bris; I imagine he did. Now here I was, sitting on an Elijah's chair, draped in my *tallit*, cradling my grandson. I cried tears of joy from the moment the baby was handed to me.

Havi has the creative gene from her Mom, so the bris was a wonderful celebration, with readings for each family member, explanations of the baby's names, songs, poems, and reflections. But it took a good forty-five minutes. The *moyel* did his business in the first few minutes, and the baby did fine, sucking on a gauze pad soaked with wine. But, forty-five minutes! Finally the service was over, and everyone erupted in song, *"Siman tov, u'mazal tov!"* I don't know what came over me, but as the singing came to an end, I stood up, held the baby high over my head, and yelled, *"Hakuna matata!"*

Did you see *The Lion King?*

Presenting the new prince of the tribe, Gabriel Elijah

The Hope of God

There are moments that stop you in your tracks, moments that bring you to the precipice of life, moments that lay bare the fears and hopes always lurking just under the surface.

As Susie and I get older, we have had our share of health issues. And I've learned an important life lesson from them: there is a thin line between hope and fear. On a Monday morning, as Susie lay on a hospital gurney awaiting a procedure to determine if she had heart trouble, my mind raced between the two emotions.

We had recently returned from a long journey overseas with visits to Hong Kong, Australia, and New Zealand. Susie had done well on the flights, but she had been unable to walk through the airports without an acute shortness of breath. I knew this was a symptom of heart disease, and I convinced her that she needed to address the problem as soon as we returned to Los Angeles. It was then that she confided in me how poorly she was feeling, yet she feared finding out the true cause.

Susie began a series of tests ordered by her doctors. Susie was a longtime type 2 diabetic, and any number of consequences of this silent disease could be contributing to her lethargy. In short order, she had an MRI of the brain, a CT scan of her gastrointestinal tract and lungs, and a series of blood tests. But after the cardiologist reviewed her electrocardiogram, the doctor forcefully recommended an immediate angiogram to investigate whether Susie had blockages in her heart arteries. And so she awaited the test that would examine the inside of her heart that Monday morning at Kaiser Permanente–Sunset.

Have you ever been in a hospital waiting room? You don't know what to hope for. And you are darn sure afraid.

As I sat in that waiting room near the heart catheterization lab, my mind vacillated between the twin poles of hope and fear. I hoped they wouldn't find anything. But then what was causing her poor health? So I hoped they would find something. And if they did find a blockage, I hoped the doctors would be able to balloon the artery, pushing the plaque against the arterial walls and opening the flow of blood to the heart. But what if they couldn't? What if they found blockages like the ones discovered in my cousin Bruce's heart a year earlier, blockages that could not be fixed with a balloon, blockages that could only be bypassed, necessitating open-heart surgery. Open-heart surgery on a fifty-eight-year-old woman, my beloved wife of thirty-eight years! I knew the risks of open-heart surgery; my father and father-in-law both had multiple heart procedures. The image of Susie with a "zipper," a scar down the middle of her chest, enduring the ventilator tube in the throat—well, it was frightening.

Sometimes you look for God in a waiting room. I prayed to ward off the fear. And I waited, and waited, and waited.

A few hours passed. Suddenly Dr. Aharonian, the head of the Kaiser heart cath lab, appeared at the entrance of the waiting room. He was dressed in green scrubs, with a white surgical mask dangling from his ears. He motioned for me to join him in the hallway.

"She's doing fine," he began. "She'll be in the recovery room for about an hour, and then you'll be able to see her. We found something ..."

My heart began to race as he continued. "Your wife has a 95 percent blockage of the ramus artery in her heart ..."

"Oh my God!" I gasped as both fear and hope grabbed me by the throat.

"... and thankfully it was in a position where we could fix it with a balloon and a stent," Dr. A continued. "She is a lucky woman. She should do well." I nearly collapsed in relief as I shook his hand and offered my thanks.

In the recovery room Susie was well aware of what had happened. She had been awake through the entire procedure, joking with the nurses, assisting the doctors as they instructed her to move in this direction or that. They even pointed out the blockage to her on a big-screen television monitor in the operating room.

I bent over the bed and kissed her on the cheek. "I love you," I whispered.

"I love you too," Susie answered. "I guess we dodged a bullet. I was heading for a heart attack."

I began to sob. "Thank God. Thank God."

After two days in the hospital Susie returned home. At our Shabbat table she said an ancient Jewish prayer, *Birkat ha-Gomel*, recited by those who have survived a danger, returned safely from a long journey, or recovered from a serious illness: "Praised are You, Lord our God, Sovereign of the universe, who graciously bestows favor upon the undeserving, even as You have bestowed favor upon me."

And as the ritual specifies, I responded, "May God who has been gracious to you continue to favor you with all that is good."

Not all prayers resonate for me, but this one captured my emotions completely. If anyone deserved God's favor, it is Susie. I only hoped that she would understand this was a shot across the bow, a warning that it was time to take seriously the health challenges she faced.

She did. She completely altered her diet. She treated her diabetes aggressively. She hired a personal trainer and began to exercise for the first time in her life. Her friends called to inquire about her recovery. I often responded, "Oh, she's focused now; she has the fear of God in her."

One day as these words escaped my lips, I caught myself. "Actually, she doesn't have the fear of God in her; she has the *hope* of God."

Hope. *Ha-tikvah.* It is the antidote to the paralysis of fear.

When I thought of writing a book that became *The Seven Questions You're Asked in Heaven*, I did some research by asking friends and family, "When you get to heaven, what do you think you'll be asked about your life on earth?" I heard the expected: "Did you make a difference?" "Were you a good person?" My mother had a different response. She thought about the question a long while and then answered, "I think I'll be asked: Were you a good daughter? A good sister? A good wife? A good mother?" And so as I think back over my life, I wonder the same thing: how did I do as a son, a brother, a husband, a father, a grandfather? The notion of a spiritual accounting of the soul—a *cheshbon ha-nefesh*—is at the heart of a life review.

This is the purpose of the High Holy Days, a ten-day period of introspection, culminating in the amazing and challenging twenty-five hours of Yom Kippur, a time of mystery, honesty, and spirituality. In the synagogue of my youth, I would enter through the back vestibule, which was lined with memorial plaques with the names of dearly departed. Next to each name was a small light bulb, which was usually turned on only on the anniversary of the person's death. But on *Kol Nidrei* (the Yom Kippur evening prayer) night, every single light bulb was illuminated, creating an eerie glow that filled the sanctuary with the memory of souls we loved.

To this day I love Yom Kippur. It is my favorite holiday. There is something absolutely transformative about the day. It is the culmination of the Ten Days of Renewal, ten days of reflecting on my life and my purpose, a period of confronting terrifying fears—"who shall live, who shall die?"—and the empowering hope that the coming year be one of good health and blessing.

On Yom Kippur I am just a little lower than the angels. In fact all of the spiritual practices of the day are designed to help me focus on my soul, not my body—to elevate me from my animal existence to something higher. On Yom Kippur I spend almost the entire day in the synagogue immersed in prayer, study, and reflection. I fast all day. I don't wear leather, a sign of luxury. I don't bathe, shave, or wear cologne. I don't have intimate relations with my spouse. She doesn't mind, because I don't bathe, shave, or wear cologne.

A neighbor of mine goes one step further: he wears a white robe called a *kittel*. It's not actually a robe; it's a burial shroud.

All of this is designed for one purpose: to encourage a personal accounting of the soul, an accounting that leads to transformation, to change, to renewal. Taken seriously, it can be a time to confront our fears and to renew our hopes.

But then at the end of Yom Kippur, I join the millions of other hungry Jews for a "break-fast." Our family tradition when I was a kid was to break the fast with orange juice. In Los Angeles I break the fast with a quick trip to my frozen yogurt place. (I eat frozen yogurt just about every day.) In Omaha the most coveted break-fast invitation is to join my cousins Don and Nancy Greenberg. More than one hundred people are invited to their beautiful home, most arriving famished from the Yom Kippur fast, eager to enjoy the incredible feast prepared by the Greenbergs.

The feast features many delicacies—Nancy's homemade blintzes, Pam Friedlander's strudel, Margo Rosen's version of Bubbie's cookies. But for thirty years the major food attraction has been the smoked fish flown in from Barney Greengrass, the "Sturgeon King" in New York City. For landlocked Jews in Omaha, the Nova lox, whitefish, and pickled herring in cream sauce are quite a treat. Once I introduced Nancy to the pleasures of pickled lox in cream sauce (a marinated filet of salmon smothered in sweet cream and sweet onions—next to *gribenes*, my favorite food *ever*!), she added this *meychel* (delightful food) to the order from Barney's. Suffice it to say, everyone lucky enough to snare an invitation to the Greenbergs' blowout Yom Kippur break-fast enjoys the permission to, excuse the expression, pig out on fish.

Once I was visiting New York City on business and arranged to have a meeting at Barney Greengrass on Eighty-Sixth and Amsterdam. After lunch I went to the front counter to pay the bill (cash only!). Sitting behind the register was a portly elderly man, dressed in a white open-collared shirt, with his head down, concentrating on the pile of bills and orders spread out on the counter. I later learned this was the irascible Moe Greengrass, the second-generation owner of Barney's. Hoping to engage him in conversation despite his obvious concern with the business at hand, I said, "Hey, you don't know me—my name is Ron Wolfson, and I'm visiting from Los Angeles—but I think you know my cousins from Omaha, Don and Nancy Greenberg."

When he heard these names, Moe slowly, slowly, slowly lifted his head, looked me straight in the eye and, with the deadpan expression of an expert comedian, uttered two words: "Good account."

Good account. The goal of Yom Kippur.

The purpose of the frightful, awe-full, and challenging moments when we face up to our fears, our frailties—both physical and spiritual—and hope to come out renewed on the other side.

Havi's wedding. *Left to right:* Dad, Mom, Me, Havi, Dave, Susie, Abe, and Michael

Keep Moving

My father-in-law, Abe, was one of the toughest guys you'll ever meet. Once he retired from his factory job at the age of sixty-five, Susie and I bought him a membership at the JCC health club in Omaha, and he worked out every day for the rest of his life.

Abe had his health issues. He had chronic asthma and emphysema. In 1993 he had open-heart surgery in Los Angeles to replace a worn aortic heart valve and bypass five arteries. The pig valve was meant to last ten years. On April 12, 2005, Abe turned ninety-five years old. We celebrated his birthday in a car—on an emergency trip to the Mayo Clinic in Rochester, Minnesota. Abe had fallen gravely ill. When Abe asked what they could do, the doctor in Omaha answered, "What do you want, Abe? You're ninety-five. Your replacement heart valve was only good for at most ten years. It's been twelve years. There's nothing more to do."

"Take me to Mayo," Abe told us. And so we checked Abe out of the hospital. While he sat slumped in the back seat, covered by a blanket, barely awake, extremely pale and getting weaker by the moment, Susie and I found ourselves driving Abe east to Des Moines on Interstate 80 and then heading north on I-35 to Minnesota. We were in a race for his life.

What we witnessed the next day in Abe's hospital room was absolutely incredible. The doctor took his hand in hers, looking carefully at his fingernails. In an instant, she looked him straight in the eye and said, "Abe, you have an infection in your heart."

A heart surgeon agreed to do a second open-heart surgery on Abe because he was in such good shape. But the infection had to be cleared up, a process that took eight weeks. You know what Abe did in those eight weeks? He bought himself a new car—and insisted on a ten-year warranty!

When we returned to Mayo for the surgery, Abe told the doctor, "Listen. I got a new car for mine ninety-fifth birthday, and I got mineself a ten-year warranty. I vant the same deal on the new heart valve!"

Abe did well, returning to the health club he loved so much. When his friends asked why he worked out so religiously, Abe told this story in his inimitable Yiddish accent: "Vell, do you know who the *malach ha-maves* is? The *malach ha-maves* is the Angel of Death. Every day, the *malach ha-maves* has a quota—he's gotta bring in a certain number of people. Now, he's a kinda lazy guy, the *malach ha-maves*; he doesn't like to work too hard. So he looks for a lazy one—someone sitting on the couch, eating potato chips, watching television. Easy catch! But if he sees that you're moving, runnin', well, he figures, 'I'm not runnin' after him. I'll catch him some other time.' So ... keep moving!"

Abe kept moving for another five years. Just after a wonderful one-hundredth birthday celebration, Abe walked into the wet steam room—his favorite place in the world—sat down, and fell asleep, and the *malach ha-maves* finally caught up with this wonderful man. On the bottom of his tombstone, we inscribed the following words: "Keep moving!"

Saying Good-bye

The first person I ever saw die was Zaydie Louie. I loved him deeply for all that he stood for: his strength, his independence, his caring for those less fortunate, his popularity as a public figure, his devotion to Jewish life. But his four packs a day of unfiltered Camels and kidney failure caught up to him, reducing him to a shadow of a man.

When it was clear the end was near, Mom called me in St. Louis to come quick. The family had camped out in the waiting room on the eighth floor, as was their tradition. I walked into the corner suite of Clarkson Hospital and there Zaydie was, prone in the hospital bed, weakened by many years of illness and totally dependent on the doctors and technologies of modern medicine. Soon, he slipped into a coma, a deep and peaceful sleep. The physicians had done all they could; the machines had been removed. Surrounded by his devoted daughters, sons-in-law, and grandchildren, Louis Paperny was about to leave this world. As he drew his last breath, an incredible calm came over his body, and I whispered the words he could not: "*Sh'ma Yisrael, Adonai Eloheinu, Adonai Echad.* Hear O Israel, *Adonai* is our God, *Adonai* is One."

I had no idea what would happen next, but what did occur was certainly nothing like the movies. No nurse came into the room to cover the body with a sheet. No doctor came in to pronounce him dead. Rather, we, his family, sat close to him, sobbing and weeping, letting the realization of the finality sink in. Zaydie was gone, and now we had to embark on the ancient rites of coping with death in the Jewish tradition, rites designed both to honor the dead and to empower the living.

In stark contrast to the weeks and months of waiting as Zaydie "slipped away," his burial would be completed in less than twenty-four hours. Within minutes of his death, the rabbi and funeral home had been contacted, a time set, an obituary written, and a lightning-fast series of phone calls made to alert the community to the news. Since all the arrangements were handled by Mom and her sisters, I felt lost and frustrated at not being able to do something to express my grief—or my love for Zaydie. Then I remembered something I had learned in my studies that enabled me to act.

I announced to my parents that I wanted to be a *shomer*, an attendant, to my grandfather's body. I wanted to go to the mortuary and stay with Zaydie throughout the night; according to Jewish practice, the deceased is not to be left alone. Traditionally people from the community are asked or hired to fulfill this act of *kavod ha-meit*, "honoring the dead." Frankly my parents had never heard of such a thing, but they quickly gave their blessing. The next thing I knew, I was at the door of the Jewish funeral home, ready to fulfill the mitzvah of *sh'mirah*.

It was the first time I had ever stepped foot in a mortuary, and to be quite honest, it gave me the shivers. The thought of spending the night in a place with a dead body was, at best, disconcerting. Yet the wonderful old man who greeted me at the door quickly dispelled any fears. He thanked me for coming. "You're a good boy to sit here with your Zaydie. It's a big mitzvah."

Suddenly I was there by myself except, of course, for Zaydie in the next room. It was an eerie feeling, but I did not feel like I was alone. I picked up a book of Psalms and began reading the Hebrew to myself. Thankfully my brothers, Bobby and Doug, decided to join me throughout the night. We reminisced about Zaydie and the truly wonderful times we spent with him.

In the middle of the night I looked at Zaydie's coffin and realized something was wrong. They had placed his body in a plain pine box, not the nicer mahogany coffin that I knew Mom and her sisters would want their beloved father buried in. In my mind's eye, I envisioned my grief-stricken mother shrieking at the first sight of this box, her anguish multiplied by her feelings of dishonoring Zaydie. It was too late to call her to ask what to do, so I acted.

"Boys," I said to Bobby and Doug. "We've got to move Zaydie from this plain coffin to a nicer one. Mom will freak out if she sees him in this. We can't wait until morning; there won't be time. It has to be done now. We have to do it. For Zaydie—and for Mom."

Both brothers shuddered at the thought, but they agreed. Carefully, slowly, we opened the plain pine box ... and there lay our Zaydie, dressed in a white linen shroud, his torn *tallit* draped around his neck, a ceremonial *kippah* on his head. He looked like a king. Through the gauze of the shroud, his face was beautiful and still, his eyes shut, his mouth turned slightly upward in a small smile.

From a storeroom, we rolled the mahogany casket parallel with the plain pine box. Carefully, slowly, we positioned our arms underneath Zaydie's lifeless body, lifted him up, and transferred him into his new, final resting place. As I closed the coffin, I kissed the top and whispered, "*Shluff*, Zaydie, *shluff*."

The time flew by, and before we knew it, morning had broken. The hearse arrived to bring the body to the synagogue for the funeral. I didn't want to leave Zaydie for a minute, so my mother had sent my suit to the funeral home and I changed there. I explained the change of casket to the funeral director, who smiled understandingly.

It is said that participating in the rituals surrounding death is the most selfless act of love in all of Jewish tradition because the deceased cannot thank you or repay your kindness. That is true, although the love and thanks I saw in Mom's eyes when we met at the synagogue for Zaydie's funeral was indeed a gift to me. Years later I had the same feeling when Michael made those matzah balls using Susie's family cookbook. It warms the hearts of parents to see their children's connection to family, to know that the Jewish values and traditions you have tried to impart to the next generation have actually been caught.

During the shiva, Mom and her sisters faced the job of distributing Zaydie's possessions to various members of the extended family. They gained great comfort in knowing that all of us grandchildren received something of meaning and memory from their home. I chose his silver cigarette lighter, the same one that was always on the side table next to his big red velvet chair. His hands were on that lighter nearly every day of his adult life. To this day when I look at it, I think of him, may his memory be a blessing.

Mom's Legacy

Three days after my mother died, I was sitting at the small blue granite breakfast table in my parents' apartment, looking through her papers with my brother Bob and his wife, Sibby. Mom had kept lists of phone numbers, bank accounts, and insurance policies in two places. One we knew about: a small blue hardcover book of blank pages given to her as a birthday present by her grandson Michael. It was there we had also found her handwritten instructions for her funeral:

> Two plots—Beth El Cemetery
> Chapel or graveside service
> Rabbi Azriel

The second place was a small blue (Mom loved the color blue) two-ring notebook Bobby had discovered in a drawer of old tax returns. The three of us were flipping through the pages, marveling at how Mom managed the finances and conducted her businesses.

Sibby, an outstanding executive assistant to senior "C-level" executives of a major international company, had offered to handle the bills, and Bobby, a lawyer by training, agreed to submit the insurance claims. "You're already doing Abe's bills," Bobby said, referring to my then ninety-nine-year-old father-in-law. "I'll take this back to New York," Sibby said as she reached for the open notebook. "I'll just put it in my purse."

As she was closing the notebook, we saw it—a small white envelope tucked into the inside front cover. It had one word on the front, written in blue ink, unmistakably in Mom's fluid hand: "*Important.*"

All three of us held our breath and looked at each other, momentarily frozen in wonderment. What could it be? Slowly, cautiously, I opened the envelope. Inside there were four small sheets of stationery, creased in half. I took them out and unfolded the papers. Across the top of each page was a printed name in flowing script: "*Bernice Wolfson.*"

I read the first few words and began to cry.

"What is it, Ronnie?" Bobby asked.

"Oh my God," I sobbed. "It's a letter from Mom." I held the small white envelope in one hand and the four pages of stationery in the other.

"We can't read this now," I said to Bobby and Sibby. "Dougie's not here. Let's wait until after the shiva tonight, and we'll read it together."

"You're right, Ronnie," Bobby said, as I put the pages back into the envelope and stuck it in my pocket.

We all wondered what it was Mom had written to us. She had written "Important" on the front. It was tucked into the flap of her notebook where she kept all the financial information. Maybe it was a revelation, perhaps where to find a secret bank account. Maybe it was a list of who should get what. Maybe it was some deep family secret she wanted us to know.

The rest of the afternoon was excruciating, with the letter sitting in my pocket, discovered but unread. I called Doug to tell him about it and that we had decided not to read it until Mom's sons could gather to hear it at the same time. I think he was grateful that we waited.

Bobby called. Mom had agreed to a biopsy test to determine the cause of her illness so we boys would know. "The results are in," Bobby said. "Pancreatic cancer."

"Oh, no," I groaned. "The worst."

"Yep, the worst," Bob replied. "They can't tell how long she had it, but I bet it was years. She always complained of stomach pain. You know what her doctor told me at the funeral? She refused all screenings for cancer, no mammograms, no colonoscopy, nothing. If she had it, she didn't want to know."

"Well," I concluded, "she gave us the gift of knowing. There's not much we can do about it, but who knows? Maybe there will be advances."

Our cousins Nancy and Don Greenberg, God bless them, had generously offered their lovely home for us to hold shiva services. After most of the guests left the house that third night, I motioned to my brothers to join me upstairs in Don's office. Slowly I retrieved the envelope from my pocket and asked the boys, "Are you ready?"

They nodded their assent. I took out the four pages of the letter and began to read:

To my dear Sons—
First of all, I love you—and I'm proud of all three of you.

I began to choke up. "I don't know if I can read this ..." I mumbled.
"You can do it, Ronnie," Bobby said. "Take your time."

As I write this, my heart fills with pride for your roles as devoted husbands and particularly your roles as wonderful fathers. This, of course, is the greatest gift a child can give a parent.

"The greatest gift," I repeated. "The greatest gift ..."

Someday when you read this you will also be reminded that, as a parent, another great gift you have given me is the comfort of knowing you care for each other and that you will be there for each other if you need to be.

"Oh my God," Dougie whispered.

I had reached the bottom line of the second page. I read the four words on the page:

My simple request is ...

I paused. What could she possibly ask of us? What was her final, "simple request"? I repeated the words before I turned to the next page:

My simple request is that you talk to each other often after your mother is no longer here to keep you posted.

Stunned, all three of us were now crying. It was classic Mom.

Please keep in touch with Doug—he has a very special challenge in his life and needs the support of people who love and understand him.

Dougie lost it. Bobby put his arm around him in a gesture of profound love and understanding.

You have filled my life with so much pleasure and the most I can wish for you is that your children do the same for you.

"Oh, Mom," I sighed, as I read the last words of the letter.

I love you Ron, Bob, and Doug and thank you for giving my life so much meaning.

It was signed, simply:

Your Mother

And then, Bernice Wolfson's three sons—the best boys in the United States of America—stood together, arms around each other, and cried tears of gratitude.

"Talk about a gift," I said, wiping away my tears. "This is the greatest gift Mom could give us. Can you believe she signed it 'Your Mother,' not 'Mom'? Now that I think about it, whenever she would call, she began the conversation with 'Ronnie, this is *your mother*.' Wow. Is she something or what!"

"She's something," Bobby sighed. "Nobody like her. Not in my lifetime."

"Look at her handwriting," I pointed out. "It's beautiful. But her notebook is filled with scribbles that you can barely read. Her handwriting went downhill these last years. I wonder when she wrote this?" I asked to no one in particular.

"I bet it was at least four, five years ago," Bobby opined.

"Well," I concluded, "whenever she wrote it, it's clear she wanted us to find it. And I'm I glad we did—what a gift! It's an ethical will; it's her message to us about what is really important. It's so brilliant. Look what she did ..."

And then, teacher that I am, I began to analyze the letter—this ethical will—from Mom: Her words are direct, her intention is clear, and the feelings reflected in the letter come from the heart. Simple but profound, the letter is structured around six themes, six messages she wanted us to hear about our relationship with her, what was important to her, what we meant to her: Mom wanted to tell us she loved us and she was proud of us. She wanted us to know we had given her a gift, but she also had a request to make of us and a hope for us. And she wanted to thank us. It's almost as if she were teaching us by example how to compose a love letter to the people who matter most in our lives. If only all of us could do this someday.

To my dear Sons —

First of all, I love you and I'm proud of all three of you. As I write this, my heart fills with pride for your roles as devoted husbands and particularly your roles as wonderful fathers. This, of course, is the greatest gift a child can give a parent.

Someday when you read this you will also be reminded that, as a parent another great gift you have given me is the comfort of knowing you care for each other and that you will be there for each other if you need to be — My simple request is

that you talk to each other often after your mother is no longer here to keep you posted.

Please keep in touch with Doug — he has a very special challenge in his life and needs the support of people who love and understand him.

You have filled my life with pleasure and the most I can wish for you is that your children do the same for you.

I love you Ken, Bob & Doug and thank you for giving my life so much meaning

Your Mother

Facing Mortality—Together

My mother's death hit me hard. She was, in so many ways, the link between Zaydie and me. She was his legacy, embodying the values that propelled his life: putting family first, building community, repairing the world, creating businesses, treating employees like relatives, keeping Jewish traditions alive. She lived on the phone, and yes, I should have called her more often to fill her insatiable appetite for news about what Susie and I were doing, how my career was unfolding. She was of the generation taught not to praise children to their face, but she would rave about them to anyone who would listen, and so I craved her approval. One day I told her I was speaking in Kansas City. "Your father and I will be there," she declared. "But, Mom," I protested, hoping to save her the trouble of a trip, "you've heard my stories more than once." She didn't miss a beat: "Ronnie, I've heard Beethoven more than once too." It was the nicest compliment ever.

Mom's death brought me face-to-face with my own mortality. I was sixty years old, in relatively good health given the stress of traveling and the pressures I inflict on myself, pouring energy into every university class and public appearance, meeting every person at the door, raising money for my projects, and writing my books. When Mom died, suddenly, quite suddenly, the grief settled in my lower back, resulting in a constant pain. Suddenly every little muscle pain in my upper body felt like an impending heart attack; there were multiple trips to the emergency room for electrocardiograms that were, thankfully, negative. It was difficult to fall asleep, my mind racing with memories and stories and images of Mom.

No one thought Dad would outlive Mom by three years, but he finally succumbed to heart failure, truly a broken heart from the loss of his "Babe." Once he decided to go into hospice, Dougie called me in Australia, where I was teaching, and we rushed to Omaha, as did Bobby and Sibby from New York City. It was only a week. One of the last things Dad said to us in the Hospice House was this: "You know what I'm most proud of? When my three sons meet, they kiss."

At his funeral I realized that Mom and Dad's generation had indeed passed on. Up next—me. It's a stark reality, one that has been building since Mom, for my fiftieth birthday present, bought me a membership in AARP. It cost her five dollars.

It's been five years now since Mom died, and I still feel the impact of the loss.

One of my doctors offered a diagnosis: "Ron, you're afraid of dying." Perhaps I am. Who isn't? I've been prescribed anxiety medication; it helps with the back pain. I go to *Yizkor* services and recite the prayers for Mom and Dad and for our baby girl, and I wonder, will my kids say the prayers for me when my time comes? I believe they will. I hope they will—not because it will do much for me, but because it will do something important for them. It will continue the legacy of memory that is the lifeblood of a family.

There is a remarkable teaching from Rabbi Eliezer in *Pirkei Avot* (2:15): *Shuv yom echad lifnei mitatach,* "Return [repent] one day before you die." Excellent idea. There is only one small problem. No one knows when that day will come. So, Rabbi Eliezer continues his teaching in *Avot d'Rabbi Natan* (chapter 15): *Kol shekein she-ya'aseh teshuvah ha-yom shemah yamut l'machar,* "Return [repent] every day, lest you die tomorrow."

Last week, a sixty-nine-year-old friend of mine dropped dead playing table tennis with his grandson. One minute he was smashing a tiny white ball, and the next minute he was collapsed on the floor. At the shiva I remarked to a colleague, "I would take that. No pain. No long, drawn-out ordeal for me or for my family. Boom—you're gone."

My colleague grimaced. "But you wouldn't be able to say good-bye to your family."

"Ah," I replied. "That's why, every day, I tell my loved ones that I love 'em. That's why I end every phone call with 'Love ya!' That's why I never go to sleep without telling Susie, 'I love you.' She says, 'I love you more.' I say, 'No way. I love *you* more.' We go back and forth, back and forth, until we finally kiss goodnight."

I am prepared. There is a list of important financial information in my desk. There is a pension fund and a savings account. We even own "property" at Mount Sinai Memorial Park in Simi Valley, California—although I may not end up there. When we told Michael that we bought cemetery plots in Los Angeles, he was mortified. "Whaaaat!" he exclaimed. "You can't be buried in Los Angeles. We all have to be together with the *mishpoche* at Beth El Cemetery in Omaha!" There is no better summary of the value of family and generational connectedness.

Dad and Mom on her eightieth birthday

Epilogue

One final true story.

Hardly a day goes by that I don't think of my grandfather, the man who called me—and called me to be—the best boy in the United States of America. It occurs to me that my Zaydie Louie was about the same age as Tevye. He too left his home in Russia with a cart full of traditions, and hopes, and dreams.

I look a little like Zaydie Louie. I have the same ruddy complexion that makes it appear I'm blushing all the time. I have his sparkling blue eyes. Some say I have his entrepreneurial spirit, his love of family, his commitment to Jewish engagement, and his deep respect for the United States of America. Like my mother, I am his legacy too, and my life has been the story of passing that legacy along to the present and future generations.

It has been a blessing and a challenge. I, along with other Jewish baby boomers, was born into a generation "between"—between the dark shadows of the Holocaust and the bright brilliance of the heroic founding of the Jewish homeland in Israel. Three of my four grandparents were immigrants to this great country, and my beloved in-laws were Holocaust survivors. My father and other first-generation American Jews sought to escape the strictures of their parents' rote religion. And we boomers have been fully shaped by America. We are what Arnold M. Eisen and Steven M. Cohen call "sovereign-self Jews," individualists who decide how "Jewish" we will choose to be, sometimes on a daily basis.* We may be nostalgic about ethnic foods, we may know one hundred Yiddish words, and we may tear up watching *Fiddler*, but we also embraced the seismic

---

* Steven M. Cohen and Arnold M. Eisen, *The Jew Within: Self, Family and Community in America* (Bloomington, IN: Indiana University Press, 2000).

changes of the turbulent 1960s; we rejected prejudice, fought for civil rights, and championed women's liberation.

And we sought to reinvent old traditions in new ways. While some of our ancestors taught us *"schwer zu sein ein Yid"* ("it's hard to be a Jew")—as it certainly was in the Russia of my grandparents and the Europe of my in-laws—it was not in the United States of America. Here in this blessed country, here in this land of freedom and choice, we have sought to craft a unique American Judaism, a joyous Judaism of inspiration and spiritual uplift. I don't want to say to my children and grandchildren, "It's easy to be a Jew"; rather, I want to say to them, "It's *wonderful* to be a Jew," for Judaism can lead you to a life of meaning and purpose, belonging and blessing.

I have thought a lot about Zaydie calling me the "best boy in the United States of America." Was Voltaire correct when he said "the best is the enemy of the good?"* If there is only one "best," does everyone else rank second? Isn't "good enough" good enough? It's true there may be only one "best picture" a year, but Zaydie understood there is never only one "best grandchild." He embodied the teaching of Rabbi Zusya, who, when facing death, told his students he was unafraid that God would ask him: "Why were you not Moses?" Zusya admitted, however: "I am afraid God will ask me: 'Why were you not Zusya?'" Why were you not the best you you could be? This is what Zaydie accomplished in telling each of us we were the best boy or best girl in the United States of America. In calling us "the best," we were called to "be the best." Aspire to be the best human being you can be. And isn't that the best goal of a life well lived?

Recently I visited Zaydie's grave in Omaha. I don't know what *you* do when you visit a gravesite, but I talk to the deceased. Not out loud—and no, I don't expect a response. I'm unsure if Zaydie's soul "hears" me, and in a way it doesn't matter. It comforts me to remember him by sharing the stories of my life as I place a stone on his marker, a reminder that I was there.

---

* *"Le mieux est l'ennemi du bien."* Voltaire, *Dictionnaire Philosophique*, 1764.

On my latest visit, I told Zaydie that I hoped the dearly departed family members were gathering in front of his heavenly big-screen TV on Sunday nights. I told him his beloved St. Louis Cardinals almost won the World Series. I brought him up-to-date on his great-grandchildren, Havi and Michael. I thought he'd be tickled that I teach about his practice of welcoming his customers at the grocery store as a model for Jewish leaders. I shared with him how thrilled I was to give the High Holy Day sermon at Omaha's Temple Israel and that I took his advice and never did become a rabbi.

And then, picturing him in my mind, remembering him in my heart, I said, "And Zaydie, guess what? I'm a Zaydie, too! Ellie is four now, and she has a brother, Gabe. He's two.

"And, Zaydie, when I see the grandkids now, I melt. Ellie Brooklyn calls me 'Zaydie.' Gabe calls me 'Zade.'

"Now I get it, Zaydie. I understand the *naches* of being a grandparent. When I put Ellie in a leg lock, and look her straight in the eye, and give her a huge, scratchy, sloppy wet kiss, and say to her, 'Ellie, you're the best girl in the United States of America!' and she adds the words, suggested by Bubbie Susie, '... and the world!' I think of you. And when I put Gabe in a leg lock, and look him straight in the eye, and give him a huge, scratchy, sloppy wet kiss, and say to him, 'Gabe, you're the best boy in the United States of America!' I think of you."

From the *bubbies* and *zaydies*, the mamas and papas, the daughters and sons, to the granddaughters and grandsons, the blessings and kisses continue.

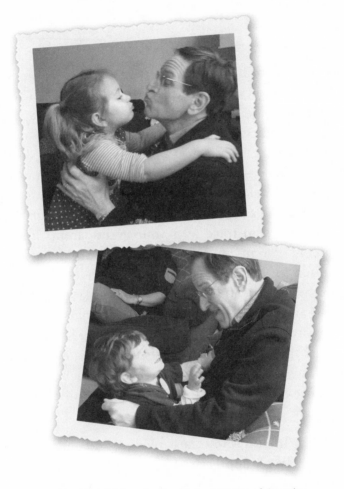

The best grandchildren in the United States of America

In Gratitude

David Brooks, brilliant author and *New York Times* columnist, observes that "individuals don't come fully formed. They emerge out of families and groups." Families especially shape personal identity, teach practical knowledge and skills, and pass down values and achievements as a legacy. Brooks writes: "The skills that go into, say, a teacher—verbal fluency, empathy, endurance—take a long time to develop. They emerge in grandparents and great-grandparents and are passed down magnified through the generations. I bet you can trace ways your grandparents helped shape your career." Parents, too, have enormous influence. In his column written for Mother's Day—"when we celebrate the powerful ways mothers shape their children"—Brooks concludes, "Some mothers—and some fathers, husbands, and wives—shape their kin with extraordinary power."[*]

I write this on Mother's Day, feeling so grateful at how my life and teaching career have certainly been influenced by the blessings of an extraordinary family and wonderful friends and colleagues. Kisses to them all, especially:

- My dear friends whose early reading and endorsement of this work is deeply appreciated.

- My brilliant editor in Jerusalem, Ilana Kurshan, whose keen eye greatly enhanced these words.

- My phenomenal publisher, Stuart M. Matlins, who enables me to tell my stories in print. Every person at Jewish Lights Publishing—Emily Wichland, Rachel Shields, Tim Holtz, Barbara

---

[*] David Brooks, "Mothers and Presidents," *New York Times*, May 6, 2015.

Heise, Leah Brewer, and Debra Hirsch Corman—is outstanding in every way.

- My friend Rabbi Moshe Rothblum, who is brilliantly directing the live presentations of *The Best Boy in the United States of America*.

- My students and colleagues at the American Jewish University, my academic home for forty years.

- The many friends I meet along the way as I continue my visits to communities near and far.

- My havurah mates: Janice and Ben Reznik, Debbie and Larry Neinstein, Bev Weise, Nan and Richard Zaitlen, Tobi and Nachum Inlender; and our Empty Nesters Shabbat group: Nessa and Jerry Naftalin, Claudia and Shlomo Bobrow, Marlene and Barry Horwitz, Jerry and Elana Scharlin, and Margaret and Paul Rosenthal, who eagerly listen to these stories, sometimes more than once.

- My cherished rabbi, Myer S. Kripke, *zichrono li'vracha*, who lived to be one hundred years old and whose wish to honor his beloved Dorothy led to the establishment of the Dorothy K. and Myer S. Kripke Institute to support the work of Jewish literacy, Jewish family education, and relational Judaism.

- My dear cousin Lottie Rosner of Sao Paulo, Brazil, and our Australian family: Ruth Bornstein, Annie and Ian Graham, Abel and Judy Bornstein, Abe and Lynne Bornstein, and their kids and grandkids.

- My wonderful extended family who are always in my heart: Aunt Ruth Luttbeg, first cousins Nancy and Don Greenberg, Bruce and Pam Friedlander, Steve and Linda Luttbeg, Laurie and Mark Spiegler, Margo Rosen, and Joan Rosen. Memories of Aunt Sylvia and Uncle Morton Friedlander, Aunt Rose and Uncle Ben Rosen, Uncle Leonard Luttbeg, Aunt Pearl and Uncle Phil Price, Uncle George Kukawka and cousins Bill and Paul Rosen—may they rest in peace—bring me smiles.

- My memories of my parents, Alan and Bernice Wolfson, my grandparents, Louis and Ida Paperny and Celia and Isadore Wolfson, in-laws Abram and Hildegarde Kukawka—*zichronam li'vracha*—will forever be a blessing.

- My brothers and their wives, Bob and Sibby and Doug and Sara; and nieces and nephews, Rebecca, Alex and Carly, Aaron and Ashley, Naomi, and Avi, who have offered me their unwavering love and support.

- You, my dear reader, who I hope enjoyed—and gleaned life lessons from—these tales. I would be thrilled to connect with you and hear your own true stories at www.bestboyintheusa.com, facebook.com/drronwolfson, or rwolfson@aju.edu.

- My beloved children, Havi and Dave, and Michael, and my grandchildren, Ellie and Gabe, who give me permission to share their stories, knowing that they are told for an important purpose. This book is my love letter to you.

- Most of all, my amazing S. K.—Susie Kukawka Wolfson—the best wife and mother in the United States of America (and the world!), the love of my life. You have blessed me beyond measure.

  Ron Wolfson

Discussion Guide

"These stories could be my stories." This is what one early reader of *The Best Boy in the United States of America* said to me. She had grown up with immigrant grandparents, a family filled with traditions and holiday celebrations, good times and sad times, and the dreams of generational continuity.

Sharing our stories is the way we define ourselves in the world. Here are some questions and activities that may help you tell your story after reading *The Best Boy in the United States of America*:

1. Which story in the book most resonated with you? Why?

2. How did your grandparents influence you? Were there other special people who influenced you?

3. Life stories can be summed up in so many different ways: "Hebrew-school-dropout turned Jewish educator" or "Nebraska boy turned Californian." How would you describe your life in one or two lines? What's *your* story?

4. What was your experience of Hebrew or religious school? Did you have a "Mr. Friedman"?

5. In the story "Bubbie's Candles," I ask, *how do we find meaning in a ritual*? Share an experience of a ritual that is meaningful to you.

6. Did you have a Bar Mitzvah or Bat Mitzvah? What memories do you have of that special occasion?

7. What's your favorite Jewish food that begins with the letter "k"? What role did food play in your family?

8. Holiday celebrations are great memory makers. Share a memory of a holiday from your youth.

9. Bring a favorite recipe or creative holiday idea to share with your group. Collect them into a booklet and copy for each participant.

10. Bonus creative idea: Make Seder fortune cookies. Wrap two small matzah crackers with a ribbon and place a "fortune" inside. Pass them out to each of your guests at the end of the evening and ask them to read their fortune out loud. The fortunes can be serious—"May we all enjoy good health!"— or funny. At Sara and David Aftergood's Seder (where we learned this idea), my fortune was: "You get to stay and help clean up this mess!"

11. What experiences have you had helping the young people in your life find true love? What do you do till the kids say "I do"?

12. Has there been a moment in your life when you struggled to overcome a personal tragedy? What helped you through it?

13. Have you ever been in a hospital waiting room? How do *you* handle the tension between hope and fear?

14. "Parents and grandparents are the most important Jewish educators our children will ever have." What are some ways you transmit your values and traditions from one generation to the next?

15. Have you written an ethical will? What process did you use? How did it feel to write a love letter to your descendants? A good resource is *Ethical Wills and How to Prepare Them: A Guide to Sharing Your Values from Generation to Generation,* edited by Rabbi Jack Reimer and Dr. Nathaniel Stampfer (Jewish Lights Publishing).

16. If you have been blessed with grandchildren, what are you called? Bubbie? Zaydie? Pappa? Grammy? Share a story about one of your best boys or best girls in the United States of America.

17. How do you shape your life to be the best you you can be?

Bible Study / Midrash

Passing Life's Tests: Spiritual Reflections on the Trial of Abraham, the Binding of Isaac *By Rabbi Bradley Shavit Artson, DHL*
Invites us to use this powerful tale as a tool for our own soul wrestling, to confront our existential sacrifices and enable us to face—and surmount—life's tests.
6 x 9, 176 pp, Quality PB, 978-1-58023-631-7 **$18.99**

Speaking Torah: Spiritual Teachings from around the Maggid's Table—in Two Volumes *By Arthur Green, with Ebn Leader, Ariel Evan Mayse and Or N. Rose*
The most powerful Hasidic teachings made accessible—from some of the world's preeminent authorities on Jewish thought and spirituality.
Volume 1—6 x 9, 512 pp, HC, 978-1-58023-668-3 **$34.99**
Volume 2—6 x 9, 448 pp, HC, 978-1-58023-694-2 **$34.99**

A Partner in Holiness: Deepening Mindfulness, Practicing Compassion and Enriching Our Lives through the Wisdom of R. Levi Yitzhak of Berdichev's *Kedushat Levi*
By Rabbi Jonathan P. Slater, DMin; Foreword by Arthur Green; Preface by Rabby Nancy Flam
Contemporary mindfulness and classical Hasidic spirituality are brought together to inspire a satisfying spiritual life of practice.
Volume 1— 6 x 9, 336 pp, HC, 978-1-58023-794-9 **$35.00**
Volume 2— 6 x 9, 288 pp, HC, 978-1-58023-795-6 **$35.00**

The Genesis of Leadership: What the Bible Teaches Us about Vision, Values and Leading Change *By Rabbi Nathan Laufer; Foreword by Senator Joseph I. Lieberman*
6 x 9, 288 pp, Quality PB, 978-1-58023-352-1 **$18.99**

Hineini in Our Lives
Learning How to Respond to Others through 14 Biblical Texts and Personal Stories
By Dr. Norman J. Cohen 6 x 9, 240 pp, Quality PB, 978-1-58023-274-6 **$18.99**

Masking and Unmasking Ourselves: Interpreting Biblical Texts on Clothing & Identity *By Dr. Norman J. Cohen* 6 x 9, 224 pp, HC, 978-1-58023-461-0 **$24.99**

The Messiah and the Jews: Three Thousand Years of Tradition, Belief and Hope
By Rabbi Elaine Rose Glickman; Foreword by Rabbi Neil Gillman, PhD
Preface by Rabbi Judith Z. Abrams, PhD 6 x 9, 192 pp, Quality PB, 978-1-58023-690-4 **$16.99**

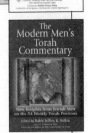

The Modern Men's Torah Commentary: New Insights from Jewish Men on the 54 Weekly Torah Portions *Edited by Rabbi Jeffrey K. Salkin*
6 x 9, 368 pp, HC, 978-1-58023-395-8 **$24.99**

Moses and the Journey to Leadership: Timeless Lessons of Effective Management from the Bible and Today's Leaders *By Dr. Norman J. Cohen*
6 x 9, 240 pp, Quality PB, 978-1-58023-351-4 **$18.99**; HC, 978-1-58023-227-2 **$21.99**

The Other Talmud—The *Yerushalmi*: Unlocking the Secrets of *The Talmud of Israel* for Judaism Today *By Rabbi Judith Z. Abrams, PhD*
6 x 9, 256 pp, HC, 978-1-58023-463-4 **$24.99**

Sage Tales: Wisdom and Wonder from the Rabbis of the Talmud
By Rabbi Burton L. Visotzky
6 x 9, 256 pp, Quality PB, 978-1-58023-791-8 **$19.99**; HC, 978-1-58023-456-6 **$24.99**

The Torah Revolution: Fourteen Truths That Changed the World
By Rabbi Reuven Hammer, PhD 6 x 9, 240 pp, Quality PB, 978-1-58023-789-5 **$18.99**
HC, 978-1-58023-457-3 **$24.99**

The Wisdom of Judaism: An Introduction to the Values of the Talmud
By Rabbi Dov Peretz Elkins 6 x 9, 192 pp, Quality PB, 978-1-58023-327-9 **$16.99**

Or phone, fax, mail or email to: JEWISH LIGHTS Publishing
Sunset Farm Offices, Route 4 • P.O. Box 237 • Woodstock, Vermont 05091
Tel: (802) 457-4000 • Fax: (802) 457-4004 • www.jewishlights.com
Credit card orders: (800) 962-4544 (8:30AM–5:30PM EST Monday–Friday)
Generous discounts on quantity orders. SATISFACTION GUARANTEED. Prices subject to change.

Congregation Resources

New Membership & Financial Alternatives for the American Synagogue
From Traditional Dues to Fair Share to Gifts from the Heart
By Rabbi Kerry M. Olitzky and Rabbi Avi S. Olitzky; Foreword by Dr. Ron Wolfson
Afterword by Rabbi Dan Judson
Practice values-driven ways to make changes to open wide the synagogue doors to many.
6 x 9, 208 pp, Quality PB, 978-1-58023-820-5 **$19.99**

Relational Judaism: Using the Power of Relationships to Transform the Jewish Community
By Dr. Ron Wolfson How to transform the model of twentieth-century Jewish institutions into twenty-first-century relational communities offering meaning and purpose, belonging and blessing.
6 x 9, 288 pp, HC, 978-1-58023-666-9 **$24.99**

The Spirituality of Welcoming: How to Transform Your Congregation into a Sacred Community
By Dr. Ron Wolfson
Shows crucial hospitality is for congregational survival and dives into the practicalities of cultivating openness. 6 x 9, 224 pp, Quality PB, 978-1-58023-244-9 **$19.99**

Jewish Megatrends: Charting the Course of the American Jewish Future
By Rabbi Sidney Schwarz; Foreword by Ambassador Stuart E. Eizenstat
Visionary solutions for a community ripe for transformational change—from fourteen leading innovators of Jewish life. 6 x 9, 288 pp, HC, 978-1-58023-667-6 **$24.99**

Building a Successful Volunteer Culture: Finding Meaning in Service in the Jewish Community
By Rabbi Charles Simon; Foreword by Shelley Lindauer; Preface by Dr. Ron Wolfson
6 x 9, 192 pp, Quality PB, 978-1-58023-408-5 **$16.99**

The Case for Jewish Peoplehood: Can We Be One?
By Dr. Erica Brown and Dr. Misha Galperin; Foreword by Rabbi Joseph Telushkin
6 x 9, 224 pp, HC, 978-1-58023-401-6 **$21.99**

Empowered Judaism: What Independent Minyanim Can Teach Us about Building Vibrant Jewish Communities
By Rabbi Elie Kaunfer; Foreword by Prof. Jonathan D. Sarna
6 x 9, 224 pp, Quality PB, 978-1-58023-412-2 **$18.99**

Inspired Jewish Leadership: Practical Approaches to Building Strong Communities
By Dr. Erica Brown 6 x 9, 256 pp, HC, 978-1-58023-361-3 **$27.99**

Judaism and Health: A Handbook of Practical, Professional and Scholarly Resources
Edited by Jeff Levin, PhD, MPH, and Michele F. Prince, LCSW, MAJCS
Foreword by Rabbi Elliot N. Dorff, PhD
6 x 9, 448 pp, HC, 978-1-58023-714-7 **$50.00**

Jewish Pastoral Care, 2nd Edition: A Practical Handbook from Traditional & Contemporary Sources
Edited by Rabbi Dayle A. Friedman, MSW, MA, BCC
6 x 9, 528 pp, Quality PB, 978-1-58023-427-6 **$40.00**

A Practical Guide to Rabbinic Counseling
Edited by Rabbi Yisrael N. Levitz, PhD, and Rabbi Abraham J. Twerski, MD
6 x 9, 432 pp, HC, 978-1-58023-562-4 **$40.00**

Professional Spiritual & Pastoral Care: A Practical Clergy and Chaplain's Handbook
Edited by Rabbi Stephen B. Roberts, MBA, MHL, BCJC
6 x 9, 480 pp, HC, 978-1-59473-312-3 **$50.00***

Reimagining Leadership in Jewish Organizations: Ten Practical Lessons to Help You Implement Change and Achieve Your Goals
By Dr. Misha Galperin 6 x 9, 192 pp, Quality PB, 978-1-58023-492-4 **$16.99**

Rethinking Synagogues: A New Vocabulary for Congregational Life
By Rabbi Lawrence A. Hoffman, PhD 6 x 9, 240 pp, Quality PB, 978-1-58023-248-7 **$19.99**

Revolution of Jewish Spirit: How to Revive *Ruakh* in Your Spiritual Life, Transform Your Synagogue & Inspire Your Jewish Community
By Rabbi Baruch HaLevi, DMin, and Ellen Frankel, LCSW; Foreword by Dr. Ron Wolfson
6 x 9, 224 pp, Quality PB, 978-1-58023-625-6 **$19.99**

*A book from SkyLight Paths, Jewish Lights' sister imprint

Children's Books

Lullaby
By Debbie Friedman; Full-color illus. by Lorraine Bubar
A charming adaptation of beloved singer-songwriter Debbie Friedman's best-selling song *Lullaby*, this timeless bedtime picture book will help children know that God will keep them safe throughout the night.
9 x 12, 32 pp, Full-color illus., w/ a CD of original music & lyrics by Debbie Friedman
HC, 978-1-58023-807-6 **$18.99** *For ages 3–6*

Around the World in One Shabbat
Jewish People Celebrate the Sabbath Together
By Durga Yael Bernhard
Takes your child on a colorful adventure to share the many ways Jewish people celebrate Shabbat around the world.
11 x 8½, 32 pp, Full-color illus., HC, 978-1-58023-433-7 **$18.99** *For ages 3–6*

It's a ... It's a ... It's a Mitzvah
By Liz Suneby and Diane Heiman; Full-color illus. by Laurel Molk
Join Mitzvah Meerkat and friends as they introduce children to the everyday kindnesses that mark the beginning of a Jewish journey and a lifetime commitment to *tikkun olam* (repairing the world).
9 x 12, 32 pp, Full-color illus., HC, 978-1-58023-509-9 **$18.99** *For ages 3–6*

Also Available as a Board Book: That's a Mitzvah
5 x 5, 24 pp, Full-color illus., Board Book, 978-1-58023-804-5 **$8.99** *For ages 1–4*

What You Will See Inside a Synagogue
By Rabbi Lawrence A. Hoffman, PhD, and Dr. Ron Wolfson; Full-color photos by Bill Aron
A colorful, fun-to-read introduction that explains the ways and whys of Jewish worship and religious life.
8½ x 10¼, 32 pp, Full-color photos, Quality PB, 978-1-59473-256-0 **$8.99*** *For ages 6 & up*

Because Nothing Looks Like God
By Lawrence Kushner and Karen Kushner
Invites parents and children to explore, together, the questions we all have about God.
11 x 8½, 32 pp, Full-color illus., HC, 978-1-58023-092-6 **$18.99** *For ages 4 & up*

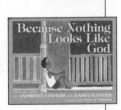

In God's Hands *By Lawrence Kushner and Gary Schmidt*
Each of us has the power to make the world a better place—working ordinary miracles with our everyday deeds.
9 x 12, 32 pp, Full-color illus., HC, 978-1-58023-224-1 **$16.99** *For ages 5 & up*

What Makes Someone a Jew? *By Lauren Seidman*
Reflects the changing face of American Judaism. Helps preschoolers and young readers understand that you don't have to look a certain way to be Jewish.
10 x 8½, 32 pp, Full-color photos, Quality PB, 978-1-58023-321-7 **$8.99** *For ages 3–6*

In Our Image: God's First Creatures
By Nancy Sohn Swartz God asks all of nature to offer gifts to humankind—with a promise that the humans would care for creation in return.
Full-color illus., eBook, 978-1-58023-520-4 **$16.95** *For ages 5 & up*
Animated app available on Apple App Store and the Google Play Marketplace **$9.99**

The Book of Miracles: A Young Person's Guide to Jewish Spiritual Awareness
Written and illus. by Lawrence Kushner
6 x 9, 96 pp, 2-color illus., HC, 978-1-879045-78-1 **$16.95** *For ages 9–13*

The Jewish Family Fun Book, 2nd Edition: Holiday Projects, Everyday
Activities, and Travel Ideas with Jewish Themes *By Danielle Dardashti and Roni Sarig*
6 x 9, 304 pp, w/ 70+ b/w illus., Quality PB, 978-1-58023-333-0 **$18.99**

When a Grandparent Dies: A Kid's Own Remembering Workbook for
Dealing with Shiva and the Year Beyond *By Nechama Liss-Levinson*
8 x 10, 48 pp, 2-color text, HC, 978-1-879045-44-6 **$15.95** *For ages 7–13*

*A book from SkyLight Paths, Jewish Lights' sister imprint

Life Cycle

Jewish Spiritual Parenting: Wisdom, Activities, Rituals and Prayers for Raising Children with Spiritual Balance and Emotional Wholeness
By Rabbi Paul Kipnes and Michelle November, MSSW
Offers parents, grandparents, teachers and anyone who interacts with children creative first steps and next steps to make the Jewish holidays and every day engaging and inspiring. 6 x 9, 240 pp (est), Quality PB, 978-1-58023-821-2 **$18.99**

Jewish Wisdom for Growing Older: Finding Your Grit & Grace Beyond Midlife *By Rabbi Dayle A. Friedman, MSW, MA, BCC* Mines ancient Jewish wisdom for values, tools and precedents to embrace new opportunities and beginnings, shifting family roles and experiences of illness and death.
6 x 9, 176 pp, Quality PB, 978-1-58023-819-9 **$16.99**

Ethical Wills & How to Prepare Them
A Guide to Sharing Your Values from Generation to Generation
Edited by Rabbi Jack Riemer and Dr. Nathaniel Stampfer; Foreword by Rabbi Harold S. Kushner
A unique combination of "what is" and "how to" with examples of ethical wills and a step-by-step process that shows you how to prepare your own.
6 x 9, 272 pp, Quality PB, 978-1-58023-827-4 **$18.99**

Grief / Healing

Facing Illness, Finding God: How Judaism Can Help You and Caregivers Cope When Body or Spirit Fails *By Rabbi Joseph B. Meszler*
6 x 9, 208 pp, Quality PB, 978-1-58023-423-8 **$16.99**

Grief in Our Seasons: A Mourner's Kaddish Companion *By Rabbi Kerry M. Olitzky*
4½ x 6½, 448 pp, Quality PB, 978-1-879045-55-2 **$18.99**

Healing and the Jewish Imagination: Spiritual and Practical Perspectives on Judaism and Health *Edited by Rabbi William Cutter, PhD*
6 x 9, 240 pp, Quality PB, 978-1-58023-373-6 **$19.99**

Healing from Despair: Choosing Wholeness in a Broken World
By Rabbi Elie Kaplan Spitz with Erica Shapiro Taylor; Foreword by Abraham J. Twerski, MD
5½ x 8½, 208 pp, Quality PB, 978-1-58023-436-8 **$16.99**

Healing of Soul, Healing of Body: Spiritual Leaders Unfold the Strength & Solace in Psalms *Edited by Rabbi Simkha Y. Weintraub, LCSW*
6 x 9, 128 pp, 2-color illus. text, Quality PB, 978-1-879045-31-6 **$16.99**

Judaism and Health: A Handbook of Practical, Professional and Scholarly Resources
Edited by Jeff Levin, PhD, MPH, and Michele F. Prince, LCSW, MAJCS
Foreword by Rabbi Elliot N. Dorff, PhD 6 x 9, 448 pp, HC, 978-1-58023-714-7 **$50.00**

Midrash & Medicine: Healing Body and Soul in the Jewish Interpretive Tradition
Edited by Rabbi William Cutter, PhD; Foreword by Michele F. Prince, LCSW, MAJCS
6 x 9, 352 pp, Quality PB, 978-1-58023-484-9 **$21.99**

Mourning & Mitzvah, 2nd Edition: A Guided Journal for Walking the Mourner's Path through Grief to Healing *By Rabbi Anne Brener, LCSW*
7½ x 9, 304 pp, Quality PB, 978-1-58023-113-8 **$19.99**

Tears of Sorrow, Seeds of Hope, 2nd Edition: A Jewish Spiritual Companion for Infertility and Pregnancy Loss *By Rabbi Nina Beth Cardin*
6 x 9, 208 pp, Quality PB, 978-1-58023-233-3 **$18.99**

A Time to Mourn, a Time to Comfort, 2nd Edition
A Guide to Jewish Bereavement *By Dr. Ron Wolfson; Foreword by Rabbi David J. Wolpe*
7 x 9, 384 pp, Quality PB, 978-1-58023-253-1 **$21.99**

When a Grandparent Dies: A Kid's Own Remembering Workbook for Dealing with Shiva and the Year Beyond *By Nechama Liss-Levinson, PhD*
8 x 10, 48 pp, 2-color text, HC, 978-1-879045-44-6 **$15.95** *For ages 7–13*

Social Justice

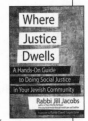

Where Justice Dwells
A Hands-On Guide to Doing Social Justice in Your Jewish Community
By Rabbi Jill Jacobs; Foreword by Rabbi David Saperstein
Provides ways to envision and act on your own ideals of social justice.
7 x 9, 288 pp, Quality PB, 978-1-58023-453-5 **$24.99**

There Shall Be No Needy
Pursuing Social Justice through Jewish Law and Tradition
By Rabbi Jill Jacobs; Foreword by Rabbi Elliot N. Dorff, PhD; Preface by Simon Greer
Confronts the most pressing issues of twenty-first-century America from a deeply
Jewish perspective. 6 x 9, 288 pp, Quality PB, 978-1-58023-425-2 **$16.99**

There Shall Be No Needy Teacher's Guide 8½ x 11, 56 pp, PB, 978-1-58023-429-0 **$8.99**

Conscience
The Duty to Obey and the Duty to Disobey
By Rabbi Harold M. Schulweis (z"l)
Examines the idea of conscience and the role conscience plays in our relationships
to government, law, ethics, religion, human nature, God—and to each other.
6 x 9, 160 pp, Quality PB, 978-1-58023-419-1 **$16.99**; HC, 978-1-58023-375-0 **$19.99**

Judaism and Justice: The Jewish Passion to Repair the World
By Rabbi Sidney Schwarz; Foreword by Ruth Messinger
6 x 9, 352 pp, Quality PB, 978-1-58023-353-8 **$19.99**

Spirituality / Women's Interest

Embracing the Divine Feminine: Finding God through the Ecstasy of
Physical Love—The Song of Songs Annotated & Explained
Annotation and Translation by Rabbi Rami Shapiro; Foreword by Rev. Cynthia Bourgeault, PhD
Restores the Song of Songs' eroticism and interprets it as a celebration of the love
between the Divine Feminine and the contemporary spiritual seeker.
5½ x 8½, 176 pp, Quality PB, 978-1-59473-575-2 **$16.99***

The Women's Haftarah Commentary
New Insights from Women Rabbis on the 54 Weekly Haftarah Portions,
the 5 Megillot & Special Shabbatot
Edited by Rabbi Elyse Goldstein
Illuminates the historical significance of female portrayals in the Haftarah and the
Five Megillot. 6 x 9, 560 pp, Quality PB, 978-1-58023-371-2 **$19.99**

The Women's Torah Commentary
New Insights from Women Rabbis on the 54 Weekly Torah Portions
Edited by Rabbi Elyse Goldstein
Over fifty women rabbis offer inspiring insights on the Torah, in a week-by-week format.
6 x 9, 496 pp, Quality PB, 978-1-58023-370-5 **$19.99**; HC, 978-1-58023-076-6 **$34.95**

The Divine Feminine in Biblical Wisdom Literature
Selections Annotated & Explained
Translation & Annotation by Rabbi Rami Shapiro; Foreword by Rev. Cynthia Bourgeault, PhD
5½ x 8½, 240 pp, Quality PB, 978-1-59473-109-9 **$18.99***

New Jewish Feminism: Probing the Past, Forging the Future
Edited by Rabbi Elyse Goldstein; Foreword by Anita Diamant
6 x 9, 480 pp, HC, 978-1-58023-359-0 **$24.99**

The Quotable Jewish Woman
Wisdom, Inspiration & Humor from the Mind & Heart
Edited by Elaine Bernstein Partnow
6 x 9, 496 pp, Quality PB, 978-1-58023-236-4 **$19.99**

*A book from SkyLight Paths, Jewish Lights' sister imprint

Inspiration

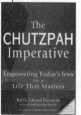

The Chutzpah Imperative: Empowering Today's Jews for a Life That Matters *By Rabbi Edward Feinstein; Foreword by Rabbi Laura Geller*
A new view of chutzpah as Jewish self-empowerment to be God's partner and repair the world. Reveals Judaism's ancient message, its deepest purpose and most precious treasures. 6 x 9, 192 pp, HC, 978-1-58023-792-5 **$21.99**

Judaism's Ten Best Ideas: A Brief Guide for Seekers
By Rabbi Arthur Green, PhD A highly accessible introduction to Judaism's greatest contributions to civilization, drawing on Jewish mystical tradition and the author's experience. 4½ x 6½, 112 pp, Quality PB, 978-1-58023-803-8 **$9.99**

Into the Fullness of the Void: A Spiritual Autobiography *By Dov Elbaum*
One of Israel's leading cultural figures provides insights and guidance for all of us. 6 x 9, 304 pp, Quality PB, 978-1-58023-715-4 **$18.99**

The Bridge to Forgiveness: Stories and Prayers for Finding God and Restoring Wholeness
By Rabbi Karyn D. Kedar 6 x 9, 176 pp, Quality PB, 978-1-58023-451-1 **$16.99**

The Empty Chair: Finding Hope and Joy—Timeless Wisdom from a Hasidic Master, Rebbe Nachman of Breslov *Adapted by Moshe Mykoff and the Breslov Research Institute*
4 x 6, 128 pp, Deluxe PB w/ flaps, 978-1-879045-67-5 **$9.99**

The Gentle Weapon: Prayers for Everyday and Not-So-Everyday Moments—Timeless Wisdom from the Teachings of the Hasidic Master Rebbe Nachman of Breslov *Adapted by Moshe Mykoff and S. C. Mizrahi, together with the Breslov Research Institute*
4 x 6, 144 pp, Deluxe PB w/ flaps, 978-1-58023-022-3 **$9.99**

God Whispers: Stories of the Soul, Lessons of the Heart *By Rabbi Karyn D. Kedar*
6 x 9, 176 pp, Quality PB, 978-1-58023-088-9 **$16.99**

God's To-Do List: 103 Ways to Be an Angel and Do God's Work on Earth
By Dr. Ron Wolfson 6 x 9, 144 pp, Quality PB, 978-1-58023-301-9 **$16.99**

Happiness and the Human Spirit: The Spirituality of Becoming the Best You Can Be
By Rabbi Abraham J. Twerski, MD
6 x 9, 176 pp, Quality PB, 978-1-58023-404-7 **$16.99**; HC, 978-1-58023-343-9 **$19.99**

Life's Daily Blessings: Inspiring Reflections on Gratitude and Joy for Every Day, Based on Jewish Wisdom *By Rabbi Kerry M. Olitzky* 4½ x 6½, 368 pp, Quality PB, 978-1-58023-396-5 **$16.99**

Restful Reflections: Nighttime Inspiration to Calm the Soul, Based on Jewish Wisdom
By Rabbi Kerry M. Olitzky and Rabbi Lori Forman-Jacobi
4½ x 6½, 448 pp, Quality PB, 978-1-58023-091-9 **$16.99**

Sacred Intentions: Morning Inspiration to Strengthen the Spirit, Based on Jewish Wisdom
By Rabbi Kerry M. Olitzky and Rabbi Lori Forman-Jacobi
4½ x 6½, 448 pp, Quality PB, 978-1-58023-061-2 **$16.99**

Saying No and Letting Go: Jewish Wisdom on Making Room for What Matters Most
By Rabbi Edwin Goldberg, DHL; Foreword by Rabbi Naomi Levy
6 x 9, 192 pp, Quality PB, 978-1-58023-670-6 **$16.99**

The Seven Questions You're Asked in Heaven: Reviewing and Renewing Your Life on Earth *By Dr. Ron Wolfson* 6 x 9, 176 pp, Quality PB, 978-1-58023-407-8 **$16.99**

Kabbalah / Mysticism

Ehyeh: A Kabbalah for Tomorrow
By Rabbi Arthur Green, PhD 6 x 9, 224 pp, Quality PB, 978-1-58023-213-5 **$18.99**

The Gift of Kabbalah: Discovering the Secrets of Heaven, Renewing Your Life on Earth
By Tamar Frankiel, PhD 6 x 9, 256 pp, Quality PB, 978-1-58023-141-1 **$18.99**

Jewish Mysticism and the Spiritual Life: Classical Texts, Contemporary Reflections *Edited by Dr. Lawrence Fine, Dr. Eitan Fishbane and Rabbi Or N. Rose*
6 x 9, 256 pp, Quality PB, 978-1-58023-719-2 **$18.99**

Seek My Face: A Jewish Mystical Theology *By Rabbi Arthur Green, PhD*
6 x 9, 304 pp, Quality PB, 978-1-58023-130-5 **$19.95**

Zohar: Annotated & Explained *Translation & Annotation by Dr. Daniel C. Matt*
Foreword by Andrew Harvey 5½ x 8½, 176 pp, Quality PB, 978-1-893361-51-5 **$18.99**
(A book from SkyLight Paths, Jewish Lights' sister imprint)

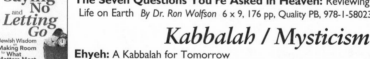

Spirituality

Amazing Chesed: Living a Grace-Filled Judaism
By Rabbi Rami Shapiro Drawing from ancient and contemporary, traditional and non-traditional Jewish wisdom, reclaims the idea of grace in Judaism.
6 x 9, 176 pp, Quality PB, 978-1-58023-624-9 **$16.99**

Jewish with Feeling: A Guide to Meaningful Jewish Practice
By Rabbi Zalman Schachter-Shalomi (z"l) with Joel Segel
Takes off from basic questions like "Why be Jewish?" and whether the word *God* still speaks to us today and lays out a vision for a whole-person Judaism.
5½ x 8½, 288 pp, Quality PB, 978-1-58023-691-1 **$19.99**

Perennial Wisdom for the Spiritually Independent: Sacred Teachings—
Annotated & Explained *Annotation by Rabbi Rami Shapiro; Foreword by Richard Rohr*
Weaves sacred texts and teachings from the world's major religions into a coherent exploration of the five core questions at the heart of every religion's search.
5½ x 8½, 336 pp, Quality PB, 978-1-59473-515-8 **$16.99***

A Book of Life: Embracing Judaism as a Spiritual Practice
By Rabbi Michael Strassfeld 6 x 9, 544 pp, Quality PB, 978-1-58023-247-0 **$24.99**

Bringing the Psalms to Life: How to Understand and Use the Book of Psalms
By Rabbi Daniel F. Polish, PhD 6 x 9, 208 pp, Quality PB, 978-1-58023-157-2 **$18.99**

Does the Soul Survive? 2nd Edition: A Jewish Journey to Belief in Afterlife, Past Lives
& Living with Purpose *By Rabbi Elie Kaplan Spitz; Foreword by Brian L. Weiss, MD*
6 x 9, 288 pp, Quality PB, 978-1-58023-818-2 **$18.99**

Entering the Temple of Dreams: Jewish Prayers, Movements and Meditations for
the End of the Day *By Tamar Frankiel, PhD, and Judy Greenfeld*
7 x 10, 192 pp, illus., Quality PB, 978-1-58023-079-7 **$16.95**

First Steps to a New Jewish Spirit: Reb Zalman's Guide to Recapturing the Intimacy &
Ecstasy in Your Relationship with God *By Rabbi Zalman Schachter-Shalomi (z"l) with Donald Gropman*
6 x 9, 144 pp, Quality PB, 978-1-58023-182-4 **$16.95**

Foundations of Sephardic Spirituality: The Inner Life of Jews of the Ottoman Empire
By Rabbi Marc D. Angel, PhD 6 x 9, 224 pp, Quality PB, 978-1-58023-341-5 **$18.99**

God & the Big Bang: Discovering Harmony between Science & Spirituality
By Dr. Daniel C. Matt 6 x 9, 216 pp, Quality PB, 978-1-879045-89-7 **$18.99**

God in Our Relationships: Spirituality between People from the
Teachings of Martin Buber
By Rabbi Dennis S. Ross 5½ x 8½, 160 pp, Quality PB, 978-1-58023-147-3 **$16.95**

The God Upgrade: Finding Your 21st-Century Spirituality in Judaism's 5,000-Year-
Old Tradition *By Rabbi Jamie Korngold; Foreword by Rabbi Harold M. Schulweis*
6 x 9, 176 pp, Quality PB, 978-1-58023-443-6 **$15.99**

The Jewish Lights Spirituality Handbook: A Guide to Understanding, Exploring &
Living a Spiritual Life *Edited by Stuart M. Matlins*
6 x 9, 456 pp, Quality PB, 978-1-58023-093-3 **$19.99**

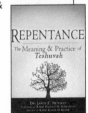

Judaism, Physics and God: Searching for Sacred Metaphors in a Post-Einstein World
By Rabbi David W. Nelson
6 x 9, 352 pp, Quality PB, inc. reader's discussion guide, 978-1-58023-306-4 **$18.99**
HC, 352 pp, 978-1-58023-252-4 **$24.99**

Repentance: The Meaning and Practice of Teshuvah
By Dr. Louis E. Newman; Foreword by Rabbi Harold M. Schulweis; Preface by Rabbi Karyn D. Kedar
6 x 9, 256 pp, HC, 978-1-58023-426-9 **$24.99**; Quality PB, 978-1-58023-718-5 **$18.99**

The Sabbath Soul: Mystical Reflections on the Transformative Power of Holy Time
Selection, Translation and Commentary by Eitan Fishbane, PhD
6 x 9, 208 pp, Quality PB, 978-1-58023-459-7 **$18.99**

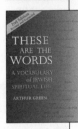

Tanya, the Masterpiece of Hasidic Wisdom: Selections Annotated & Explained
Translation & Annotation by Rabbi Rami Shapiro; Foreword by Rabbi Zalman Schachter-Shalomi (z"l)
5½ x 8½, 240 pp, Quality PB, 978-1-59473-275-1 **$18.99***

These Are the Words, 2nd Edition: A Vocabulary of Jewish Spiritual Life
By Rabbi Arthur Green, PhD 6 x 9, 320 pp, Quality PB, 978-1-58023-494-8 **$19.99**

**A book from SkyLight Paths, Jewish Lights' sister imprint*

About Jewish Lights

People of all faiths and backgrounds yearn for books that attract, engage, educate, and spiritually inspire.

Our principal goal is to stimulate thought and help all people learn about who the Jewish People are, where they come from, and what the future can be made to hold. While people of our diverse Jewish heritage are the primary audience, our books speak to people in the Christian world as well and will broaden their understanding of Judaism and the roots of their own faith.

We bring to you authors who are at the forefront of spiritual thought and experience. While each has something different to say, they all say it in a voice that you can hear.

Our books are designed to welcome you and then to engage, stimulate, and inspire. We judge our success not only by whether or not our books are beautiful and commercially successful, but by whether or not they make a difference in your life.

For your information and convenience, at the back of this book we have provided a list of other Jewish Lights books you might find interesting and useful. They cover all the categories of your life:

Bar/Bat Mitzvah	Life Cycle
Bible Study / Midrash	Meditation
Children's Books	Men's Interest
Congregation Resources	Parenting
Current Events / History	Prayer / Ritual / Sacred Practice
Ecology / Environment	Social Justice
Fiction: Mystery, Science Fiction	Spirituality
Grief / Healing	Theology / Philosophy
Holidays / Holy Days	Travel
Inspiration	Twelve Steps
Kabbalah / Mysticism / Enneagram	Women's Interest

Stuart M. Matlins, Publisher

Or phone, fax, mail or email to: **JEWISH LIGHTS** Publishing
Sunset Farm Offices, Route 4 • P.O. Box 237 • Woodstock, Vermont 05091
Tel: (802) 457-4000 • Fax: (802) 457-4004 • www.jewishlights.com
Credit card orders: **(800) 962-4544** (8:30AM–5:30PM EST Monday–Friday)
Generous discounts on quantity orders. SATISFACTION GUARANTEED. Prices subject to change.